Making Change Happen in Student Affairs

Challenges and Strategies for Professionals

Margaret J. Barr
George S. McClellan
and Arthur Sandeen

JB JOSSEY-BASS™
A Wiley Brand

Contents

Preface

McClellan and Stringer observe, "Change has arguably served as the metatheme for student affairs since the 1960s" (2009, p. 623). They go on to suggest several needed changes in student affairs professional practice in the future. One of their suggested changes is "an energetic focus on student learning as the essential component of student affairs practice, dissolving barriers between student affairs and academic colleagues on many campuses, and emerging models of both organization and practice" (p. 623). Another is recognition and appropriate adaptation of student affairs programs and services to "the centrality of technology in their [students'] lives, higher numbers of students with serious mental health concerns, increasingly diverse student populations, and the need to redefine traditional notions of what 'student development' entails, both in theory and in practice" (pp. 623–624). Like McClellan and Stringer, the authors of *Envisioning the Future of Student Affairs*, a report from a task force jointly commissioned by the American College Personnel Association (ACPA) and the National Association of Student Personnel Administrators (NASPA), note that change in student affairs is situated within the broader context of continuing change in the broader contexts of higher education and society. "As in all fields of higher education in the United States, student affairs has been influenced by shifting social, economic, and political trends in its ever changing environment"

(ACPA and NASPA, 2010b). Our goal in writing this book is to present a set of concepts or strategies student affairs professionals working in a continuously changing environment might use in addressing the challenges and opportunities they face on their campuses in their field.

We have identified seven concepts or strategies to include in our discussion. They are using foundational documents and ethics; applying theory, literature, and data to practice; managing resources; utilizing technology; advocating for students; fulfilling our responsibilities as educators; and reframing our professional practice. These concepts or strategies are addressed in the first seven chapters of the book. The eighth and final chapter offers concluding thoughts.

Each chapter offers what we hope will be helpful information, illustrative case studies (adapted from actual events at campuses around the country) with discussion, and reflective questions we hope will guide our readers in considering their own work.

The concepts and strategies were chosen based on our experiences as professionals and scholars in student affairs. We also chose them because we believe they are relatively timeless, meaning that they have served and will continue to serve student affairs professionals well even as the circumstances and contexts of our professional practice shift. These are not the only seven concepts or strategies that can or should be used; they are the seven that we find enduring, powerful, and useful.

This book reflects our collective thinking regarding leading change, but one or another of us served as primary author for each chapter. It is not surprising, therefore, that there are differences in style and voice between the chapters. Given our feeling that this book is a somewhat personal reflection of our experiences and perspectives, we have chosen to honor those individual distinctions rather than trying to blend them as one might in a work intended to reflect a more neutral or impersonal narrative.

Our audience for this work includes student affairs professionals at all points of the career span. This includes senior student affairs officers, mid-managers, and entry-level professionals. It may also be useful to presidents, provosts, and others who supervise student affairs divisions without an extensive background in the field. Another audience will be graduate students, particularly those who are finishing their formal coursework and preparing to take positions of leadership in student affairs. Naturally we hope the book will be seen as useful to faculty in graduate preparation programs both as it relates to their efforts in preparing practitioners and in their role as scholars contributing to the study of higher education.

Why this book? There are a number of resources available to student affairs professionals, graduate student faculty, and others in higher education related to management issues in our profession. Most of the literature, however, focuses on the issues and not on specific strategies that might be used by the active student affairs professional seeking to solve ongoing issues and problems. It is our hope that our work here will help fill this void and will provide a valuable resource for colleagues. As was the case in our earlier collaboration, "it would be presumptuous of us to claim that we have the answers" (Sandeen and Barr, 2006, p. xii). Our attempt here is not to be proscriptive with regard to addressing particular issues or opportunities but instead to describe strategies for analysis from multiple perspectives as a way of developing a plan of action that is timely and focused on the unique characteristics of the institution where the professional works.

Why now? The challenges and opportunities available to those lucky enough to serve students in higher education are remarkable. Simply put, we believe there has never been a more exciting or interesting time in which to be a student affairs professional. This volume is a call to action on the part of our colleagues to apply what we as a profession know from our shared foundations, from theory, and from practice to confronting and solving the problems facing higher education and our students.

Acknowledgments

Margaret (Peggy) Barr thanks her friends and colleagues at Northwestern University, Texas Christian University, and Northern Illinois University, who helped her learn each day as she served as a vice president. She also would like to thank those who have supported her through both good and challenging times, including Sheila Driscoll, Sharon Justice, Carolyn Krulee, John Dunkle, Mickie Emmett, and Denise Rode. She also appreciates the support of her family, which has grown smaller in recent years but nevertheless is close across the generations. Finally, she thanks both Art Sandeen and George McClellan for being good professional partners in this enterprise and excellent friends.

George McClellan thanks his students and colleagues at Indiana University–Purdue University Fort Wayne for the challenge, inspiration, and support they so generously share with him. Particular thanks to Chancellor Vicky Carwein, Danita Davis, and Chad Richmond for their support. He is grateful for the gift of friendship from Peggy Barr, Ken Christmon, Mary Jo Gonzales, Steve Grud, Jason Laker, and Joe Minonne, who help him up on the tough days, help him celebrate on the good days, and try to help him be humble most days. Finally, he is honored to have been invited to serve as coauthor with two people—Peggy Barr and Art Sandeen—who have helped shaped him as a student affairs professional and scholar and who have had a significant, positive influence on the field we love.

Art Sandeen is indebted to his friends and colleagues in NASPA, who have taught him so much about student affairs for many years. He also thanks the students at the four universities with which he has been affiliated: Miami University (O); Michigan State University, Iowa State University, and The University of Florida. His belief in higher education's transformative ability is now being happily affirmed by the current enrollment of his grandchildren. He wishes them well. He expresses his thanks to John Lombardi, Robert A. Bryan, and W. Robert Parks for their encouragement and lessons in leadership.

We are all grateful to David Brightman, Aneesa Davenport, Alison Knowles, and Erin Null, from Jossey-Bass. All authors hope to be lucky enough to have an amazing editorial team like you. We are thankful that we actually do.

About the Authors

Margaret J. Barr served as vice president for student affairs at Northwestern University from 1992 until she retired in 2000. She currently is professor emeritus in the School of Education and Social Policy at that institution. She also served as vice chancellor for student affairs at Texas Christian University (1985–1992) and vice president for student affairs at Northern Illinois University (1982–1985). Prior to becoming a senior student affairs officer she held positions as assistant vice president for student affairs at Northern Illinois University (1980–1982), associate dean of students at the University of Texas at Austin (1979–1980), and assistant dean of students at the University of Texas at Austin (1971–1979), and various student affairs positions at Trenton State College and the State University of New York at Binghamton.

She was active in the National Association of Student Personnel Administrators (NASPA), including service as director of the Richard F. Stevens Institute for Chief Student Affairs Officers (1989, 1990), president of the NASPA Foundation Board, and member of the committee that wrote "A Perspective on Student Affairs" issued on the fiftieth anniversary of the *Student Personnel Point of View*. Barr received the NASPA Outstanding Contribution to Literature and Research (1986) and the NASPA Outstanding Contribution to Higher Education Award (2000). She was named a Pillar of the Profession by the NASPA Foundation (2000) and received the Distinguished Achievement Award from the NASPA Foundation (2012).

She was also active in the American College Personnel Association (ACPA), where she served as president (1983–1984). She was named a Senior Scholar (1986–1991) and received both the Professional Service Award (1991) and the Contribution to Knowledge Award (1990) from that association.

She is the author or editor of *Budgets and Financial Management in Higher Education* (2011) with George McClellan; *Critical Issues for Student Affairs: Challenge and Opportunities* with Arthur Sandeen (2006); *An Academic Manager's Guide to Budgets and Financial Management* (2002); *A Handbook for Student Affairs Administration* (1993, and 2000 with Mary Desler); coeditor of *New Futures for Student Affairs* with M. Lee Upcraft (1990); and *Student Services and the Law* (1988) and *Developing Effective Student Service Programs* with L. Keating (1985). In addition, she served as editor-in-chief of the monograph series *New Directions for Student Services* (1986–1998).

Barr received a bachelor's degree in elementary education from the State University College at Buffalo (1961), a master's degree in college student personnel from Southern Illinois University Carbondale (1963), and a PhD in educational administration from the University of Texas at Austin (1980).

She lives in Evanston, Illinois. Barr is a member of the Evanston Women's Board of the Northwestern University Settlement Association and serves on the Board of Directors of the Settlement Association.

George S. McClellan serves as the vice chancellor for student affairs and enrollment management at Indiana University–Purdue University Fort Wayne (IPFW). Prior to joining the IPFW community, McClellan served as vice president for student development at Dickinson State University, interim director of assessment and research for Campus Life at the University of Arizona, and director of graduate and off-campus housing at Northwestern University.

He is active in both NASPA and ACPA, including currently serving as a member of the editorial board for NASPA's *Journal of College and Character* and having served in a similar role for a number of years for ACPA's *Journal of College Student Development.* McClellan also served on the NASPA Foundation board during that group's successful campaign to increase its endowment to $1M and was named in 2010 as a Pillar of the Profession by the NASPA Foundation and received the Outstanding Contribution to Higher Education Award from NASPA Region IV-East in 2012. In addition, McClellan is a past recipient of ACPA's Outstanding Contribution to Research in American Indian Higher Education award.

McClellan is author or editor of *The Handbook for College Athletics and Recreation Management* (2012) with Chris King and Don Rockey; *Stepping Up to Stepping Out: Preparing Students for Life After College* (2012) with Jill Parker; The *Handbook for Student Affairs Administration* (2009) with Jeremy Stringer; *Budgets and Financial Management in Higher Education* (2011) with Margaret Barr; *In Search of Safer Communities: Emerging Practices for Student Affairs in Addressing Campus Violence* (2008) with Peggy Jablonski and colleagues; *Ahead of the Game: Understanding and Addressing Campus Gambling* (2006) with Tom Hardy and Jim Caswell; and *Serving Native American Students in Higher Education* (2005) with Maryjo Tippeconnic Fox and Shelly Lowe. He is the author of a column in the *Chronicle of Higher Education* on career issues in student affairs and has authored numerous other articles and chapters on subjects related to student affairs.

McClellan earned his PhD in higher education from the University of Arizona (2003). Both his MSEd in higher education (1998) and BA in English and American literature (1982) were earned from Northwestern University.

He lives in Fort Wayne, Indiana. Nothing interests him more than students and higher education, though professional football and any sports team from Chicago are not far behind.

Arthur Sandeen served as professor of educational leadership at the University of Florida from 1973 until 2004 and returned to his faculty position on a half-time basis, serving until 2014. He previously served as vice president for student affairs at the University of Florida (1973–1999). Prior to his service in Florida, Sandeen held the roles of associate dean (1967–1969) of students and dean of students (1969–1973) at Iowa State University, as well as associate director of residence hall programs (1965–1967) at Michigan State University.

Sandeen was elected President of NASPA in 1977. In 1987, he chaired the committee that wrote *A Perspective on Student Affairs*, commemorating the fiftieth anniversary of *The Student Personnel Point of View*. Sandeen received the Fred Turner Award in 1982 for contributions to NASPA, the Scott Goodnight Award from NASPA in 1990 for outstanding performance as a dean; and NASPA's award for contribution to the literature in 2000. In 2014, he was the recipient of the John L. Blackburn Distinguished Service Award from the NASPA Foundation. Sandeen was a member of the 1999 inaugural class of those named by the NASPA Foundation as Pillars of the Profession.

He is the author of *Enhancing Leadership in Colleges and Universities* (2011); *Critical Issues in Student Affairs: Challenges and Opportunities* (2006) with Margaret Barr; *Enhancing Student Engagement on Campus* (2003); *Making a Difference: Profiles of Outstanding Student Affairs Leaders* (2001); *Improving Leadership in Student Affairs Administration* (2000); *The Chief Student Affairs Officer: Leader, Manager, Mediator, Educator* (1991); and *Undergraduate Education: Conflict and Change* (1976). Sandeen is also the author of three monographs, over fifty published articles, and twenty-one book chapters.

Sandeen earned his BA degree in psychology and religion in 1960 from Miami University (O), his MA in student affairs administration in 1962 from Michigan State University, and his PhD in higher education in 1965 from Michigan State University. In 1982 he was a Fulbright scholar in West Germany and in 1984 completed the Institute for Educational Management program at Harvard University.

Sandeen and his wife live in Gainesville, Florida. They have two daughters and five grandchildren. His hobbies include playing squash, reading about the U.S. Civil War, and fly fishing.

The Jossey-Bass Higher
and Adult Education Series

Using Foundational Documents and Ethics in Our Work

Solving problems and confronting issues and conflicts are routine parts of the day for most student affairs administrators. Sometimes the problems appear to be insignificant to an observer, but the resolution of the issue is important to the person or persons involved. Sometimes the issue is a long-standing one with no easy answers and requires patience, fortitude, research, and reflection on the part of student affairs· administrators as they try to find a satisfactory conclusion. Sometimes the issue appears to be new and perplexing but upon reflection there are strategies and solutions that have been tried before that might provide guidance and help to the practitioner. Sometimes the problem or issue merely needs someone to recognize an issue and become involved in developing a solution with the parties concerned about it. Sometimes it appears that the problem is unsolvable or there is no easy or satisfying solution for all the parties involved.

Sometimes, however, a problem that surfaces again and again is an indicator that a fundamental change needs to happen in the way we approach problem solving. It is in times like these that revisiting our foundational documents can help practitioners gain perspective, see the issue through a different set of lenses, and gain insight into possible solutions to difficult issues and concerns. It is at these perplexing times that we need to revisit our foundations as a profession and our reasons for engaging in this work.

This chapter reviews the documents that provide the foundation for our professional practice in student affairs by articulating the values embraced by student affairs professionals. In addition, it presents case studies that focus on how these ideas and constructs influence our decision making on a day-to-day basis. Finally, the chapter concludes with reflective questions for the reader to consider regarding how they might more actively use these resources to help them confront the issues faced by active student affairs professionals every day.

Our Foundational Documents

There are many resources in the literature that can provide guidance and direction to contemporary student affairs professionals. The authors chose to trace the philosophic roots of the profession through examination of the statements supporting the student personnel point of view. Others might choose other documents that undergird the foundations of student affairs. Examples of such documents include the work of the Council on the Advancement of Standards (CAS 1986 to 2012); the *Student Learning Imperative* (American College Personnel Association [ACPA], 1996); *Principles of Good Practice in Student Affairs* (ACPA/National Association of Student Personnel Administrators [NASPA], 1997); or *Learning Reconsidered: A Campus-Wide Focus on the Student Experience* (Keeling, 2004). All of these documents illustrate the wealth of thought and ideas that are available to provide perspective while dealing with the day-to-day opportunities and challenges inherent in student affairs.

The authors believe that three seminal documents, the two iterations of *The Student Personnel Point of View* published by the American Council on Education in 1937 and 1949 and *A Perspective on Student Affairs* (NASPA 1989) provide the most timeless and relevant foundations for our shared professional practice. Each document is reflective of the time when it was written but all contain enduring values that support and explain the work of student affairs on the contemporary college or university campus.

The Student Personnel Point of View, 1937

Interest in the personnel movement at colleges and universities began in the early 1920s and was based on the work of Walter Dill Scott, who eventually became president of Northwestern University. He hired L. B. Hopkins to establish the first personnel office at Northwestern (Biddix and Schwartz, 2012, p. 285). Scott believed that "The primary purpose of college training, away and beyond that of imparting a certain amount of factual knowledge, is that of producing changes in the behavior and thinking of students. Every hour of the week, within class and without, should contribute to this underlying purpose" (Scott, 1936, p. 92). That philosophy was unusual for the time but took root and grew at Northwestern and other institutions.

In January 1925, a conference on vocational guidance was held with fourteen higher education institutions represented at the meeting (Biddix and Schwartz, 2012, p. 291). After the conference, with support from the Rockefeller Foundation, a national survey was conducted to determine the extent that the personnel methods espoused by Walter Dill Scott and L. B. Hopkins were actually being used at colleges and universities across the country. The results of the survey indicated that although there was interest in the approach of Scott and Hopkins, there was little knowledge about how to implement such programs at an institutional level (Biddix and Schwartz, 2012, p. 291).

The American Council on Education (ACE) responded by establishing five committees to explore issues of record keeping, achievement testing, personality measurement, occupational information needs, and personal development of students. Over the next several years these committees helped clarify issues and concerns of the personnel movement, but it was not until the ACE subcommittee on Student Personnel Work, including Esther Lloyd Jones, and W. H. Cowley, convened that real progress was made (Biddix and Schwartz, 2012, p. 292). The result was the publication of *The Student Personnel Point of View* (SPPV) in 1937.

Karen Pennington, in a video produced by NASPA on the occasion of the seventy-fifth anniversary of the SPPV, said it best: "*The Student Personnel Point of View* provides a context to what we do" (NASPA, 2012). The SPPV has endured over the years, because it provided an easily understood strong foundation for our professional practice.

The SPPV opens with a philosophic statement of education saying, in part, that

> One of the basic purposes of higher education is the preservation, transmission, and enrichment of the important elements of culture: the product of scholarship, research, creative imagination, and human experience. It is the task of colleges and universities to vitalize this and other educational purposes as to assist the student in developing to the limits of his potentialities and in making his contribution to the betterment of society.
>
> This philosophy imposes upon educational institutions the obligation to consider the student as a whole— his intellectual capacity and achievement, his emotional make up, his physical condition, his social relationships, his vocational aptitudes and skills, his moral and religious values, his economic resources and his aesthetic appreciations. It puts the emphasis, in brief, upon the development of the student as a person rather than upon his intellectual training alone. (NASPA, p. 49, 1989)

The focus on the student as a whole person including intellectual, personal, and interpersonal growth provides the philosophical foundation for student affairs as a professional specialty within higher education. While the specific offices or agencies included under the student affairs organizational umbrella may differ from institution to institution, *The Student Personnel Point of View* clearly states two principles for the professional work of student affairs: the need to focus on the growth and development of the whole student and the need to cooperate and coordinate efforts to focus the individual student's "total characteristics and experiences rather than with separate and distinct aspects of his personality or performance" (NASPA, 1989, p. 54).

The manner by which these two principles are implemented requires that student affairs administrators assume leadership for cooperative enterprises in the contemporary college campus. The opportunities are many and the barriers to such endeavors may be large, but *The Student Personnel Point of View* provides a firm foundation for student affairs professionals to help others understand the importance of a focus on the entire student experience as a prime educational responsibility for contemporary colleges and universities.   *importance of whole person*

The Student Personnel Point of View, 1949

World War II brought massive changes to the social structure within the United States and clarified the importance of the involvement of the United States in broader world issues and concerns. Those changes prompted the American Council on Education (ACE) to review the 1937 SPPV statement. The new committee was headed by E. G. Williamson and also included Cowley and Lloyd Jones from the original committee. After consultation and debate, a revision of the original document was published. A major change in emphasis occurred in this version with regard to the purpose of higher education by stating clearly that "preservation, transmission and enrichment of culture" was not just *one of* the basic purposes of higher education in the 1937 statement but was instead *the* basic purpose (emphasis added) of higher education in the 1949 statement (Rhatigan, 2000, p. 17).

In addition, the committee presented three additional goals for higher education:

> Education for the fuller realization of democracy in every phase of living
>
> Education directly and explicitly for international understanding and cooperation
>
> Education for the creative imagination and trained intelligence to the solution of social problems and to the administration of public affairs (NASPA, 1989, p. 21).

Influencing society and the relationships between and among nations was acknowledged as an important goal of higher education in the United States.

Further, the committee stated that "the full maturing of each student—cannot be attained without interest in and integrated efforts toward the development of *each and every facet of his personality and potentialities*" [emphasis added] (NASPA, 1989, p. 22).

In a later section, the document asserts the following:

> But such broad-gauge development of the individual should in no sense be considered as a sufficient and complete goal in itself. It is axiomatic today that no man lives in a social vacuum. Rather individual development is conditioned by the kind of society in which a person lives, and by the quality of interpersonal and group relationships which operate around him. (NASPA, 1989, p. 25)

Thus the 1949 version of the statement provides support for two important facets of student affairs practice. First, understanding that the background of the student as well as the totality of the learning environment available to the student will influence his or her success. Second, by emphasizing the link to broader purposes beyond the academy, a foundation is laid for efforts by student affairs professionals to connect students they serve with the broader society through community service, service learning, study abroad, and faith initiatives.

The 1949 SPPV then lists the following principles that should guide student affairs, including helping the student in orientation to college, academic achievement, providing satisfactory living facilities, helping students feel a part of the institution, and promoting physical fitness. In addition, the 1949 SPPV emphasized the importance of aiding students in their understanding of emotions, developing interests, enhancing learning, mastering personal financial management, progressing toward vocational goals, developing individually in a responsible manner, finding ethical and spiritual meaning, and developing "satisfying and socially acceptable sexual adjustments" (NASPA, 1989, p. 34). The final responsibility for student affairs outlined in the 1949 SPPV is to help the student prepare for "satisfying and constructive post college activity" (NASPA, 1989, p. 34). The addition of these underlying principles reinforces the necessity of providing health services, counseling services, and career services as an essential part of the responsibility of student affairs on any college campus.

Further, the 1949 statement concludes with strong recommendations to centralize the administration of student affairs (NASPA, 1989) and emphasizes the need to have active participation by student personnel staff and students in the administration of the institution (NASPA, 1989). In addition, for the first time this version of *The Student Personnel Point of View* states that students should be directly involved in evaluating staff, assessing the quality of current services, and suggesting new services (NASPA, 1989).

Finally, the 1949 SPPV concludes with a strong case for ongoing evaluation of programs, services, and student experiences and urges continuing research on student needs and development, stating: "The effectiveness of a student personnel program is determined not solely by either its technical quality or its administrative and financial structure but even more by its institutional setting" (NASPA 1989, p. 44). The statement rejects the notion that one size fits all with regard to what services and programs should be part of student affairs but asserts the important role the institutional president has in setting the mores of the campus and thus guiding student development (NASPA, 1989).

The 1949 document is a powerful statement and is often overlooked by professionals in student affairs. Although the language often may seem antiquated, for example, referring to the student only using the masculine pronoun, it clearly asserts the need for centralization of student personnel services and involvement of student personnel professionals in the administration of the institution, and it supports the connection between the institution and the broader local, national, and international society

A Perspective on Student Affairs, 1987

President Judith Chambers of NASPA convened the Plan for a New Century Committee chaired by Arthur Sandeen. The committee represented a broad range of student affairs professionals from a range of institutional types and professional roles. Among the members were those who had served in leadership positions in both ACPA and NASPA. The committee conducted eighteen public forums during the year that they worked and received input through correspondence, calls, and email from a wide range of student affairs professionals. The result of this process and committee deliberations was a final report called A *Perspective on Student Affairs*. Both the committee and NASPA were clear that this was not a revision of either the 1937 or 1949 statements but rather a "perspective written in 1987 to stimulate greater understanding of student affairs among leaders in higher education" (NASPA, 1989, p. 2).

When describing the 1987 context of higher education the committee said: "The traditional purposes of higher education are to preserve, transmit, and create knowledge, to encourage personal development, and to serve society. In addition, college and university programs help individuals cope with significant life transitions—from adolescence to adulthood, from dependence to personal autonomy, from one occupation to another. Technological advances and escalating rates of change add to the complexity and challenge associated with these transitions" (NASPA, 1989, p. 9). The statement goes on to describe the many changes in the student body of American higher education, including but not limited to gender, race, national origin, sexual orientation, marital status, veteran status, and age—changes that continue to this day.

The committee described, in detail, the assumptions and beliefs that undergird the work of student affairs. The report clearly says that "No one of these assumptions and beliefs is unique to student affairs. Indeed, they are held by many others in higher education. It is the combination of these assumptions and beliefs that is distinctive. Together they define the special contributions made by student affairs" (NASPA, 1989, p. 11).

The assumptions and beliefs that guide the statement are

"The academic mission of the institution is preeminent;

Each student is unique;

Each person has worth and dignity;

Bigotry cannot be tolerated;

Feelings affect thinking and learning;

Student involvement enhances learning;

Personal circumstances affect learning;

Out-of-class environments affect learning;

A supportive and friendly community life helps students learn;

The freedom to doubt and question must be guaranteed;

Effective citizenship should be taught; and

Students are responsible for their own lives." (NASPA, 1989, pp. 11–14)

Recognizing that "the character of an institution largely determines the nature of student affairs programs, therefore organizational structures and services may vary widely from one campus to another" (NASPA, 1989, p. 15), acknowledgment is given to the many and varied organizational structures and reporting relationships for student affairs. In addition, the document emphasizes that the beliefs and knowledge of student affairs staff influence the manner in which they work. Further, it concludes that "student affairs staff should be expected to be experts on students and their environments" (NASPA, 1989, p. 15). Also the statement emphasizes the need for student affairs professionals to take leadership in the resolution of campus disputes and problems and use their knowledge base and expertise to encourage open communication and problem resolution. It also reminds institutions and professionals that "In a pluralistic campus community the manner in which policies are made, decisions are reached and controversial issues are handled may be as important as the results themselves. Indeed, an institution transmits values to students by the way it approaches policies, decisions and issues" (NASPA, 1989, p. 15). This admonishment to pay attention to process when approaching problem solving is important to all practicing professionals. Additionally, student affairs professionals are reminded that they have an obligation to advocate for and help establish "open and humane methods of campus decision-making and the rational resolution of conflict" (NASPA, 1989, p. 15). Attending to process does not mean that decision making should be ponderous and slow. The pace of the change on the contemporary college campus dictates decisions also need to be made in a timely manner.

The statement then provides a listing of a number of programs and services that student affairs provide both directly to institutions and directly to students. Throughout the extensive list emphasis is placed on coordination with other offices and agencies, as well as focusing on being good managers of the resources available to them to help students grow and develop.

Affirming that student affairs staffs serve both the institution and students, the statement also describes the difficult role that they play on many college campuses. Providing the sense of balance between individual rights and freedoms and the common good is important for students to learn while they are members of a learning community so that they can use that knowledge as they take their place in the broader society. A *Perspective on Student Affairs* concludes with the following statement:

> Student affairs has a diverse and complicated set of responsibilities. As a partner in the educational enterprise, student affairs enhances and supports the academic mission. In addition student affairs professionals must advocate for the common good and champion the right of the individual; encourage intelligent risk taking and set limits on behavior; encourage independent thought and teach interdependent behavior. The extent to which colleges are successful in creating climates in which these paradoxical goals can coexist will be reflected in how well students are able to recognize and deal with such dilemmas during and after college (NASPA, 1989, p. 19).

These three statements provide a helpful guidance to the practicing student affair professional. By providing both a foundation and framework to guide decision making, they continue to serve the profession. All clearly emphasize the need for student affairs professionals to assume leadership to resolve conflicts and open communication with students, with others within the institution, and with stakeholders beyond the institutional boundaries. Those tasks are not easy, and they are further complicated by the obligation of student affairs professionals to adhere to the ethical standards of our shared profession as we make decisions and implement policies.

Our Ethical Responsibilities

Making ethical decisions is central to the effectiveness of student affairs work. Treating others as we would like to be treated is essential to being regarded as an ethical person. Our effectiveness is based on the trust that students and others place in us. Trust is earned through consistent, ethical behavior. Trying to identify both the intended and the unintended consequences of a decision is an excellent first step for any student affairs professional faced with an ethical dilemma.

Each student affairs professional has personal ethical standards developed through our relationships with families, our interactions with others, our teachers, and our religious beliefs. Our institutions also have ethical standards to which we must also adhere. In addition, as student affairs professionals, we also have ethical standards to uphold from our chosen professional associations.

Karen Kitchener (1985) synthesized five ethical principles that have been adopted by many professional organizations and provide the foundation for their statements of ethical responsibilities for members. They include the following: respecting autonomy, doing no harm, helping others, being just, and being trustworthy (Kitchener, 1985). Her work provided an easily understood framework for student affairs professionals to use when faced with ethical issues. Dalton, Crosby, Valente and Eberhardt (2009) declare that "Managing ethics is more an art than a science" (p. 160). They have extended the understanding of ethical issues by defining five domains or areas where student affairs professionals have responsibilities. Those domains include student welfare, the institution, the profession, the community, and personal conscience (2009, pp. 169–171).

Each of the student affairs professional associations have ethical standards that describe the behavior that is expected from each member of the organization. Four of those ethical statements have been chosen to illustrate the guidance such standards can give to student affairs professionals as they go about their daily work. Those standards are the CAS *Statement of Shared Ethical Principles* (Council for the Advancement of Standards, 2006); *Statement of Ethical Principles and Standards* (ACPA, 2006); the *Standards of Professional Practice Statement* (NASPA, 1990); and ACPA *and* NASPA, *Professional Competencies Areas for Student Affairs Practitioners: Ethical Professional Practice* (2010a). All are presented here, as they differ slightly in emphasis and content.

CAS Statement of Shared Ethical Principles

The Council for the Advancement of Standards (CAS) includes thirty-five professional organizations. Their ethical statement affirms that CAS respects the ethical codes of each of the member organizations and does not intend to "replace or supplant the code of ethics of any professional organization; rather it is intended to articulate those shared ethical principles" (CAS, 2006). The CAS Statement articulates seven principles that member organizations and consequently their members should follow. Those principles are closely linked to those stated by Kitchener and, in fact, CAS acknowledges Kitchener in a footnote to their statement (CAS, 2006).

The principles are

- Autonomy: We take responsibility for our actions and both support and empower an individual's and group's freedom of choice.

- Non-Malfeasance: We pledge to do no harm.

- Beneficence: We engage altruistic attitudes that promote goodness and contribute to the health and welfare of others.

- Justice: We actively promote human dignity and endorse equality and fairness for everyone.

- Fidelity: We are faithful to an obligation, trust or duty.

- Veracity: We seek and convey the truth in our words and actions.

- Affiliation: We actively promote connected relationships among all peoples and foster community (Council for the Advancement of Standards, 2006).

The CAS statement of ethical standards concludes with the following statement, saying in part that "When professionals act in accordance with ethical principles, program quality and excellence are enhanced and ultimately students are better served" (CAS, 2006).

Although broad, the CAS ethical principles provide excellent guidelines for ethical practice by student affairs professionals. They rely on the ethical principles identified by Kitchener and do not conflict with the ethical standards of the member professional organizations. When accepting the CAS Standards for specialty areas in student affairs, institutions implicitly also adopt the shared ethical standards of CAS.

American College Personnel Association Ethical Principles and Standards

ACPA's Ethical Principles and Standards (ACPA, 2006) provide additional guidance for student affairs professionals who wish to act in an ethical manner. In addition to stating the ethical principles of the association, the document provides background on the ethical foundations that support the standards and additional information about the principles in extensive appendices. ACPA has approached the issue of ethical principles and standards by stating broad standards with a comprehensive explanatory statement under each standard. The four standards of ACPA include professional responsibility and competence, student learning and development, responsibility to the institution, and responsibility to society.

Professional Responsibility and Competence

With regard to the ethical obligation to be a responsible and competent practitioner, the ACPA document states:

> Student affairs professionals are responsible for promoting and facilitating student learning about students and their world, enhancing the quality and understanding of student life, advocating for student welfare and concerns and advancing the profession and its ideals. They possess the knowledge, skills, emotional stability, and maturity to discharge responsibilities as administrators, advisors, consultants, programmers, researchers, and teachers. High levels of professional competence are expected the performance of these duties and responsibilities. Student affairs practitioners are responsible for their actions or inaction. (ACPA, 2006)

The ACPA ethical statement clearly states that failure to act in situations with ethical dimensions is a violation of the ethical standards of the association.

Student Learning and Development

ACPA identifies support for student learning and development as an ethical responsibility by noting that

> Student development is an essential purpose of higher education. Support of this process is a major responsibility of the student affairs profession. Development is complex and includes cognitive, physical, moral, social, emotional, career, spiritual, personal and intellectual dimensions. Professionals must be sensitive to and knowledgeable about the variety of backgrounds, cultures, experiences, abilities, personal characteristics, and viewpoints evident in the student population and be

> able to incorporate appropriate theoretical perspectives
> to identify learning opportunities and to reduce barriers
> to development. Multicultural competence is a funda-
> mental element of ethical practice. (ACPA, 2006)

Specific guidance is then provided to professionals on how to apply
the standards to the issues confronted in their professional lives.

Responsibility to the Institution

ACPA also outlines the ethical obligation to one's institution,
saying in part that

> Institutions of higher education provide the context for
> student affairs practice. Institutional mission, goals, pol-
> icies, organizational structure and culture, combined
> with individual judgment and professional standards
> define and delimit the nature and extent of practice.
> Student affairs professionals share responsibility with
> other members of the academic community for fulfilling
> the institutional mission. Responsibility to promote the
> development of students and to support the institution's
> policies and interests require that professionals balance
> competing demands. (ACPA, 2006)

The emphasis in this document on ethical responsibilities to the
institution where the student affairs professional is employed is
explicit. It should be actively considered by members in their daily
professional practice.

Responsibility to Society

ACPA affirms that student affairs professionals have ethical responsibilities to society:

> Student affairs professionals both as citizen and pra-
> ctitioner have a responsibility to contribute to the

improvement of the communities in which they live and work and to act as advocates for social justice for members of those communities. They respect individuality and individual differences. They recognize that our communities are enhanced by social and individual diversity manifested by characteristics such as age, culture, class, ethnicity, gender, ability, gender identity, race, religion and sexual orientation. Student affairs professionals work to protect human rights and promote respect for human diversity in higher education. (ACPA, 2006)

At the conclusion of the standards, the ethical statement of ACPA provides suggestions on what to do if a member observes a violation of these ethical standards, and then it provides specific definitions of terms used throughout the document. The ACPA document has numerous specific standards that can serve as guideposts to the professional, helping them to not only recognize ethical issues but also to resolve those issues in a responsible and caring manner.

NASPA Standards of Professional Practice

The NASPA ethical statement (NASPA, 1990) is much less detailed than that of ACPA and focuses on the responsibilities of professionals to students and the institutions where professionals work.

NASPA (Student Affairs Administrators in Higher Education) is an organization of colleges, universities, agencies and professional educators whose members are committed to providing services and education that enhance student growth and development. The Association seeks to promote student personnel work as a professional which requires personal integrity, belief in the dignity and worth of individuals, respect for individual differences and diversity, a commitment to service, and dedication to the development of individuals and the college community through education. NASPA supports student personnel work by providing opportunities for members to expand knowledge and skills through professional education and experience. (NASPA, 1990)

The seventeen responsibilities for all members include

- Supporting the educational interest, rights, and welfare of students

- Subscribing to the general mission and goals of the institution when accepting employment

- Managing institutional resources effectively

- Assessing programs and services to assure congruence with institutional and departmental mission and goals as well as effectiveness

- Honoring employment relationships

- Providing clear and accurate position descriptions and regular performance evaluations

- Recognizing and avoiding situations where a conflict of interest may arise

- Acknowledging all lawful authority; executing professional responsibilities with fairness and impartiality

- Promoting responsible behavior and fostering conditions where students accept responsibility for their own behavior

- Ensuring all information conveyed to others is accurate and appropriate

- Ensuring that confidentiality is maintained with respect to all privileged and confidential records

- Complying with the guidelines involving research with human subjects

- Accurately representing their own professional credentials

- Supporting nondiscriminatory and fair employment practices

- Providing accurate and complete information when serving as a reference

- Promoting a sense of community

- Participating in ongoing professional development (NASPA, 1990)

The NASPA standards for ethical conduct are easy to understand. They place the responsibility for compliance on the members of the organization, including the individual professional and those who supervise professionals.

ACPA and NASPA Professional Competencies for Student Affairs Practitioners

A product of the Joint Task Force of NASPA and ACPA, *Professional Competencies for Student Affairs Practitioners* (2010a), codified specific competency expectations for student affairs professionals in the following areas: advising and helping; assessment, evaluation, and research; equity and diversity and inclusion; history, philosophy, and values; law, policy, and governance; human and organizational resources; leadership; personal foundations; student learning and development and ethical professional practice.

The competency expectations for ethics in professional practice in student affairs provide further guidance for professionals. In contrast to other statements and standards, by professionals, these expectations are based on the level of experience and knowledge of the professional involved. "These levels should not be confused with one's years of service in the field, nor with one's current positional title. Rather, the levels of basic, intermediate and advanced correspond only to the skills and attitudes one can demonstrate to others at a given point in time" (ACPA/NASPA, 2010a, p. 6).

For example, the competency expectation at the Basic Level, the professional should be able to "Describe the ethical statements and the foundational principles of any professional association directly relevant to their work" (ACPA/NASPA, 2010a). At the Intermediate Level they should be able to "Explain how one's professional practice also aligns with one's personal code of ethics and ethical statements of professional student affairs associations" (ACPA/ NASPA, 2010a), and at the Advanced Level the professional should be able to "Actively engage in conversation with staff about the ethical statements of professional associations" (ACPA/ NASPA, 2010a). The stage approach to understanding and applying ethical standards is consistent with developmental theory and is helpful to both practitioners and their supervisors.

Another illustration may help to clarify the use of the stages of development in this professional standards document. At the Basic Level the professional should be able to "Assist students in ethical decision making and make referrals to more experienced professionals when appropriate" (ACPA/NASPA, 2010a). When at the Intermediate Level of ethical development the professional should be able to "Address and resolve lapses in ethical behavior among colleagues and students" (ACPA/NASPA, 2010a). At the Advanced Level the professional should be able to "Engage in effective consultation and provide advice regarding ethical issues with colleagues and students" (ACPA/NASPA, 2010a).

This document provides specific guidance to both the individual professional working on his or her own ethical development and to those who supervise professionals. The stage approach to resolving ethical issues is helpful to both supervisors and those being supervised. It is easily accessible on the website of both associations and provides specific guidance for everyday ethical decision making at whatever stage of development the individual professional happens to be.

There is a great deal of commonality among the ethical standards of ACPA and NASPA and the ACPA and NASPA Professional Competencies document. Each student affairs professional needs to adhere to and develop an ethical philosophy that guides his or her work and relationships with colleagues, students, supervisors, and supervisees. All student affairs professionals should take responsibility to surface ethical dilemmas and have open and frank discussions about issues of concern. Most ethical issues can be resolved through such discussions, but those that cannot should be confronted and may deeply influence career paths and professional relationships.

Case Studies

Philosophical foundations and ethical standards are only valuable when they are used to address the real-life issues that student affairs professionals encounter in their day-by-day work with students, colleagues, parents, alumni, and other stakeholders in higher education. The next section provides some examples, some big and some small, that illustrate the value and use of these foundational documents in everyday student affairs practice. If the foundational documents are understood, believed, and integrated into the thought processes and actions of the student affairs professional, they can provide valuable perspective and can shape responses to real-life issues.

The Annoying Student Athlete

Everything seemed to be progressing normally during the fall semester when the director of undergraduate residential life came to the dean of students to request that a varsity student athlete student be immediately removed from his current residence hall and be banned from all on-campus housing. The freshman football player in question played his music at all hours at very high volume, which was disturbing to other residents in the building. The student resident assistant (RA) discussed the issue with the student athlete and with his roommate, who did not see the music as a problem, and eventually issued three noise violation notices, which had no impact on his behavior.

After the fourth noise violation the student athlete was asked to meet with the hall director. At that meeting he agreed to turn down the volume and apologize to the other residents. After three days of relative silence the volume increased again. The other students on the floor were fed up and talked to the RA about housing officials giving the athlete special treatment just because he is a varsity athlete. The situation was rapidly deteriorating and the director of residential life and the hall staff were at their wit's end.

The dean decided to meet with the student before making a decision about whether to ban the student from all university housing. Before that meeting the dean reviewed the background of the student athlete. He had been homeschooled until his junior year in high school and played sports through the local recreation center. His parents, upon urging from his coach, decided that the best option for him to get a scholarship for college was for him to play football at the local high school. He was not consulted about the change but went along because he felt his parents knew best. Although he played football successfully and was an asset to the team, he never fit in at the local high school. Social groups were already formed and high school was a lonely experience. He was heavily recruited and received a coveted athletic scholarship and came to XYZ University, where he was assigned to a residence hall and a roommate and was living away from home with a roommate for the first time in his life.

The dean started the meeting by asking him how he liked living in a residence hall. He responded that it was OK but he liked living at home better. At home he could play his music any way he wanted to and no one complained. His Mom and Dad were at home but they both worked in the evenings when he normally played his music to relax. The dean of students spent some time with the young man and found under the façade of a successful football player was a young man who had never lived away from home and had no idea how to live in a residence hall with other people.

The dean decided to give him another chance and spent some time with the student athlete jointly developing a list of the expectations for his behavior in any residential setting. They both signed the document and he promised to comply in his daily life. He also agreed that the dean could share her decision with the hall staff. He was also placed on disciplinary probation for two semesters. Before finalizing the decision the dean decided to meet with the RA, hall director, and director of residential life to explain her decision. At this meeting the staff expressed frustration with the decision but understood the reasoning of the dean.

At the end of the current semester the student athlete moved to another residence hall and that gave him a chance to start over; which he did. He never had another violation of any kind and at graduation he showed the dean the list which he had folded up and carried in his wallet. He told her he pulled it out whenever he thought he was going off course.

Discussion. In this situation, the dean had taken the time to deal with the whole student, listened to his whole story, and helped him understand his responsibilities as a member of a residential community. The change strategy was focused primarily on one student, although other students benefited from his changed behaviors. He was also held responsible for his unacceptable behavior but the sanctions were not what the staff directly involved wanted. The dean demonstrated that she understood the frustrations of the residence hall staff and took the time to explain her decision to them. That action demonstrated respect for the residential staff by explaining her rationale for the decision and opening the door for continued dialogue on similar issues.

Balancing Conflicting Values

Saints University is a well-known Roman Catholic institution with a strong set of traditions and a very explicit set of values, including opposition to abortion. A financial aid advisor approached the director of student financial aid with a dilemma. A student she had worked with for over two years approached her and asked her for an emergency loan of $500. The student was well known to the advisor for they had developed a warm relationship during the times she came into the office. As part of the procedure for granting an emergency loan the advisor asked the student why she needed the money. She replied that her grandmother was ill, then looked at the advisor and burst into tears.

As she cried, she told the financial aid advisor that she was pregnant and had decided to get an abortion. She did not have the funds to do it and the student insurance program did not cover the procedure. The young woman said she just could not lie to the advisor but did not know where else to go to get the rest of the needed funds so that she could proceed with her plan.

The financial advisor felt she was dealing with a situation beyond her experience and competency and did not know what to do. She told the student she would check and see what she could do and she should come back tomorrow. The advisor approached the director of financial aid and explained the situation. She knew that emergency loans were granted for unexpected circumstances such as the cost of transportation to go home for a sick or dying relative. She also knew that the institution did not support abortion as an alternative and thus it would not be an appropriate use of emergency loan funds. But she also knew she was dealing with a student who faced a difficult situation and had asked for her help.

The director told her that an emergency loan could not be granted for that purpose. But he did not stop there. He said that this was not the first time this has happened, and he pulled out a list of community agencies that could be of help to the young woman.

[handwritten: exploring campus contacts/resources/advice.]

Some were pro-life and some supported medically necessary abortion. He urged the advisor to encourage the young woman to do two things: first talk to someone in the counseling center to assure that she had really explored all alternatives available to her and second to visit the community agencies and see if any of them could be of help to her.

The advisor met with the student the next day. She had called the counseling center and talked to a staff member she knew and got the names of several staff members who had dealt with similar situations. She assured the young woman that she had not given her name to the person she talked to and had merely asked for information about experienced therapists at the center. The advisor also gave the student the list of community agencies and urged her to visit them and seek advice and help. Finally, she told her that the emergency loan fund was not available for the purpose she described because that purpose conflicted with one of the fundamental values of the institution. After she walked with the student over to the counseling center she returned to her office wishing she had done something more to help a student in distress. *[handwritten: hmm . . .]*

Discussion. Understanding the limitations of her skills, the financial aid advisor sought outside help and understood her ethical responsibilities to both the institution and to the student. Although she did not solve the problem faced by the student she considered the whole student and provided both support and information to the student. The director of financial aid understood the ethical dilemma she faced and helped her by giving her timely and helpful information. Finally, to ensure that such ethical conflicts were recognized, a change was made in the orientation program for new staff in the Financial Aid Office to include discussion of the staff members' ethical obligations to both students and the institution. Ignoring such conflicts is not helpful to either staff or students but discussing them and reinforcing what can be done while meeting the standards of the institution is useful and helpful to staff members.

To Dine or Not to Dine

The first semester was going well for the new vice president for student affairs (VPSA). The only area he was really concerned about was the food service operation. The institution had run food service through a contract to an outside vendor. The current contract concluded at the end of May. In the past, there had always been an almost automatic renewal of the contract for another three-year period. The new vice president felt there were other options available to the institution that would bring in more money to campus and, more importantly, provide better service and options for students. Yearly satisfaction surveys submitted by students resulted in dining services receiving substantially lower scores in each of the past five years.

Last month he requested that the director of dining services send the vendor a formal notice of intent by the institution to seek new bids for dining services. A small committee was in the process of developing the bid documents and students were involved in the process. Requests for proposals were almost ready for distribution to the current vendor and other food service companies across the country.

For many years it had been a tradition at the university for the vice president for student affairs, the director of housing, and the director of dining services and their spouses to be treated to a lavish dinner during the holiday season by the food service vendor. The vice president had heard about this tradition when he interviewed for the position and made a note to discuss this tradition with the parties involved. He forgot about the dinner until the invitation for him and his spouse landed on his desk.

He was reviewing his mail when the director of housing came in for his regular meeting. The director of housing noticed the invitation to dinner from the vendor on the VPSA's desk and his face lit up. He began to tell the VPSA what a lovely evening it was and how the y went to the best place in town and told the vice president how much his spouse would enjoy the evening. He went on to say how much those who participated enjoyed the evening and the staff were excited because the vendor opened up the occasion to several other people on the staff.

The vice president gently stopped the director of housing and said this was something they needed to talk about. Reminding the director that the institution was going out to bid on the food service contract, he discussed the possibility of the dinner being viewed as a conflict of interest. He stated that for the sake of the institution and the students they needed to assure the community and other vendors that the bidding process was fair and open. With that in mind he asked the director of housing to set up a meeting with all those on the staff who had been invited to the dinner this year.

At the meeting the VPSA made it clear that he would decline the dinner invitation and explained his reasons and why he saw it as an ethical breach. He said that since it had never been discussed before he would leave it up to each professional to decide if they would participate this year. In addition, he made it clear that in the future, no matter which vendor it was, the staff of the institution would not participate in such dinners.

Discussion. The vice president for student affairs dealt with two elements of change. One was based on data regarding student experience with the current dining services and his own evaluation of quality. That resulted in the decision to enter an open bidding process with vendors for a new contract. The current vendor could submit a proposal but changes in the quality of dining services needed to occur under a new contract.

The second dealt with the ethics of accepting a perk from a vendor. Having dinner with a vendor at the expense of the vendor could cloud the issue of whether or not the bidding process was open and genuine. The vice president decided that that tradition had to stop but understood the concerns of the staff involved. It was a difficult situation for the new vice president but he tried to balance competing interests. In the end some of the staff decided not to participate in the dinner this year, and others did participate. The question remains for each reader whether or not they would make the same decision the new vice president made.

Responding to an Emerging Student Population

The vice president for student affairs had become increasingly aware of the growing number of recent veterans returning to XYZ College. Their numbers are increasing each year, yet the institution has done nothing to either honor their presence among the student body or have a consistent response to the issues they were facing upon return to school. Recently a series of separate events highlighted her concern about the needs of the veteran student population. In one case, a veteran student lost patience with an academic advisor in the School of Engineering and began swearing and shouting when he felt he was not getting a straight answer to the question he asked regarding how many credits did he need to graduate. In a second case, three weeks ago one of the directors in student affairs found a veteran in tears outside the financial aid office. Her husband had not paid child support for the last two months and her rent check was due the next day. She tried to get an emergency loan but found that the money would not be available until next week. The student did not know what she should do. In a third case, a veteran who was working on the grounds crew to help pay for his education came to work one day to find his job had been eliminated in the recent budget cuts from the state and he was at a loss on how to pay his bills and feed his family.

When she brought her concerns about the institutional response to veterans up at her regular meeting with the directors in student affairs, each one had a story involving a veteran student and a problem the student faced. When she joined the academic deans at their regular meeting they echoed the need for assistance in helping veteran students. At her next meeting with the president she mentioned the need for the institution to develop a more coordinated and helpful approach to this emerging population. She presented the data regarding the number of veteran students enrolling and the number of issues involving veteran students that occurred in recent months. The president responded that the budget was tight, new programs were not going to be funded, and he did not really want to hear anything more about the issue. He looked at her and told her that she was resourceful and would figure out something.

As the problems and concerns continued to occur throughout the institution, the office of the vice president for student affairs became an informal clearing house for veteran's issues. She knew that having an informal clearinghouse was not the long-term answer, but she kept her focus on veteran students. The annual retreat for vice presidents and deans was scheduled for the next month. She knew at each meeting there was an open session where people could bring up issues not covered on the agenda. She decided to develop a proposal for a cross divisional task group to study what the real needs of veteran students were and how the institution could best respond to them. She knew that several of the academic deans would support her proposal.

The retreat occurred and at the open part of the meeting she presented her proposal. She found outstanding support from the academic deans and several of the other vice presidents. The proposal passed and the task force was formed. The day after the retreat she met with the president who was not pleased that she brought up the issue at the open meeting. He told her bluntly not to blindside him again. She told him that was not her intent but she felt that veterans' concerns were an issue that needed to be addressed. The president said he doubted that the task force would come up with anything and repeated that she should not ever blindside him like that again.

She left the meeting feeling very conflicted. On one side, she had disappointed the president, who was crucial to her career aspirations, and on the other side, she did what was right and needed for the institution. Her dilemma is not unique in higher education. The task force met and developed a shared responsibility response to veterans that involved many offices on campus, with one person in each office assigned prime responsibility for veterans' issues. The staff in governmental relations highlighted a grant opportunity that was recently approved on the federal level, and the task force decided to apply for the grant to fund their fledgling efforts. The president approved of this step and was pleased with the initial response from the task force.

Discussion. Change is sometimes difficult to accomplish and involves taking risks. Obviously the president was not pleased with the choice the vice president for student affairs made. However, the solution she proposed did not ask for new resources but focused on whether the needs were real and what could be done with the resources available to the institution. A cross divisional approach made the issue an institutional issue instead of one limited to the Division of Student Affairs.

Conclusion

The documents that provide the foundation for our profession and the ethical parameters for our work shape what we do, who we serve, and how those services are presented and performed. It is up to each student affairs professional to define for themselves the issues that are important, the risks they are willing to take, and the consequences they are willing to bear. Each professional in student affairs must make decisions each and every day that influence the lives of students, staff, and colleagues across the institution. How we make our decision is just as important as the decisions we make. We can read our foundational documents and the ethical statements of our professional associations, but if we do not integrate the principles embedded in them into our day-by-day decision-making processes they are useless to us.

Our foundational documents have a clear message to all of us: consider the whole student at all times in what we do and what we propose to do. Develop programs and services that contribute to the education, growth, and development of our students. Be purposeful in our activities and programs and help students integrate their learning into the essential fabric of their lives. At the same time we must be careful in our zeal to solve problems and make sure that we do not breach ethical boundaries in what we do. No matter what professional association is involved, the underlying principles as outlined by Kitchener (1985) remain the same. The authors would like to add one more principle to consider: think before you act of both the intended and unintended consequences of your decisions. This last step can often provide a needed perspective on the problem faced and the decisions that need to be made.

In the cases presented, reframing the issues involved brought about change in an individual student, in the orientation and training of staff, in considering the ethical implications of actions taken and not taken, and in changing an institution's response to an emerging student population. Change happens in both big and small ways, and our foundational documents can help us guide that change.

Reflection Questions

1. Consider the cases presented: would you have made the same decisions that the dean, director, or senior student affairs officers made in each case? Why or why not?

2. In each case what other issues do you see and how would you begin to resolve those issues?

3. What is the most difficult ethical issue you have faced in your professional practice? What happened? With the advantage of hindsight, would you now make a different decision?

4. What strategies can you use to bring active use of the foundational documents and ethical statements into your decision-making process?

5. Did you agree with the vice president in the last case when she ignored the explicit instructions of the president? What other strategies could she have used to develop a broad institutional response to an underserved population?

2

Applying Theory, Literature, and Data to Practice

Chapter 1 addressed using student affairs' foundational documents and ethics in our work. This chapter discusses the use of theories, professional literature, and data from research and assessment. Together, foundational materials, theories, literature, and data might be thought of as our field's intellectual resources.

This is not a chapter on theories, literature, or data per se. Readers interested in more comprehensive review of specific theories or bodies of theory might consider the work of Evans, Forney, Guido, Patton, and Renn (2010) or chapters from the theory section of *Student Services: A Handbook for the Profession* (Schuh, Jones, and Harper, 2011) among other sources. The sources of professional literature are abundant, though we will put in a word of encouragement here for including literature from more cutting-edge sources (for example, blogs) when considering what to make time to read. With regard to data (or collecting and analyzing data), Creswell's (2013) book on research design offers a terrific starting off point. One cannot go wrong when drawing on insights from Upcraft and Schuh (1996), Banta (2002), or Erwin (1991) relative to assessment.

The foundational documents and ethics of the student affairs profession discussed in Chapter 1 are by their nature relatively fixed with regard to content. On the whole, action in this arena comes through modest revisions, interpretation, or application of their content. In contrast, theory is more fluid. New theories surface, and existing theories are affirmed, modified, or discarded. Literature and data are perhaps the most dynamic elements, with new material coming forward constantly from a wide variety of sources. However, as with the foundational materials, the power of theory, literature, and data is only fully realized when brought to bear on making a difference in the success of our students, institutions, or communities.

Uses of Theory, Literature, and Data

The ways in which theory, literature, and data may be useful in our practice are similar. Among them are

- Understanding observed circumstances and behaviors

- Informing a response to a rapidly emerging opportunity or challenge

- Developing, implementing, and assessing appropriate programs and services

- Identifying and articulating a counter-narrative to prevailing or hegemonic beliefs

In addition to these uses, literature and data offer the additional use of identifying promising practices, raising questions about other practices, and debunking dated or doubtful practices. As with theory, taking full advantage of the potential of literature and data can come through either one's own review and application or through sharing the information with others for consumption and application.

Journals, reports, books, and conferences or workshops offer ready access to theory, literature, and data. Social media and the Internet make it more possible than ever for authors or publishers to share their work with those who may have an interest and opportunity to make use of it.

Looking within the Discipline

When consulting theory, literature, and data related to their professional practice, the first thought of many in student affairs is to look at work within the field. For example, Bean and Metzner's (1985) model of attrition among nontraditional students provides student affairs professionals at community colleges and regional public institutions (as well as others working with substantial numbers of such students) with a very useful framework for understanding and addressing retention. An aspiring or new senior student affairs officer reflecting on their leadership skills and professional relationships might consult the work of Rutkosky (2013) on the ways in which trust in senior leaders is developed and maintained. A newer professional seeking to better understand the experience of Christian students in faith-based student organizations would find research by Magolda and Gross (2009) to be insightful. A director hired to develop a first-year experience program can provide faculty members with a valuable and concise introduction to student development by sharing Skipper's (2005) monograph on student development in the first year. As these examples illustrate, there is an abundance of strong intellectual resources in our field upon which we in student affairs can draw in our practice.

Looking Across Disciplines

Because student affairs is a broad and interdisciplinary profession, we are also able to draw on research and literature in a variety of disciplines in higher education, including communications, cultural studies, education, psychology, sociology, and others. A student affairs professional teaching a career success course can draw on Bandura's (1977) social learning theory by including job shadowing and interviewing opportunities with professionals in fields of interest as important components of the course. A thoughtful student affairs professional reflecting on their work as an educator but concerned with the way *education* is being constructed in the professional discourse can find reinforcement and inspiration in cultural studies and critical thinking as expressed in Giroux's (1992) thoughts on pedagogy as cultural production. A graduate student seeking to understand whether and how the various professional organizations in student affairs might offer different benefits and opportunities could frame their considerations in terms of Schein's (1985) sociological writings regarding organizational cultures. A student group advisor can share Bolman and Deal's (1997) ideas on reframing organizations, which are rooted in leadership studies and organizational development, as part of their orientation program for new student leaders. An interdisciplinary perspective, an open mind, and an active reading list make it more likely that a student affairs professional will successfully draw on literature, research, or data from outside the field.

Looking Across the Map

The increasingly networked nature of our daily lives means that the context of our practice is at once local, national, and international. The Cooperative Institutional Research Program's annual study of students new to college (Higher Education Research Institute, 2013) can offer valuable information to a new professional interested in understanding students on their campus and how they compare to students at other campuses across the United States. A faculty member in a graduate preparation program may share insights into the ways in which policymakers are thinking about higher education as reflected in the American Association of State Colleges and Universities' (2013) report on public higher education. The work of Kell and Vogl (2008) arguing for a reconceptualization of international higher education could be helpful to a senior student affairs and enrollment manager office preparing to engage colleagues in a conversation about their university's international education programs. Student affairs professionals at all points in their career interested in supporting LGBTQ students or in creative approaches to professional development would do well to review the work of Allen, Edmonds, Parker, and Bach (2012). In this amazingly interconnected communication and information environment, the pool from which useful information or promising practices can be drawn is no longer limited to the local watering hole.

Theory: Not Just for Graduate School Any More

The reality of student affairs professional practice for many, however, is that they do not feel they can take time, make time, or have support from supervisors for reviewing and discussing theory as an integral and ongoing part of decision making (Evans, Forney, Guido, Patton, and Renn, 2010). Listing reasons student affairs practitioners may not make greater use of theory, Patton and Harper (2009) identified the following misperceptions: theory is boring; classic theories are useless in contemporary contexts; simply knowing theory ensures its use in practice; and "theory" was a course taught in graduate school.

However, paraphrasing a tagline from a long ago marketing campaign, theory is not just for graduate school any more. Given the growing complexity of professional practice in student affairs, the diversity and sophistication of students we serve, and the heightened expectations various constituencies have of our institutions with regard to accountability and the value of higher education, it is arguably the case that it is more important now than ever before for a student affairs practitioner to be current in their knowledge of the field's intellectual resources, including theory. An informed practitioner may more readily spot opportunities to shape programs and services in ways that add value to the student experience, identify barriers to student success, or support campus and community engagement in ways that foster citizenship and leadership.

Reading Is Fundamental—Writing, Too

MacKinnon, Broido, and Wilson (2004) observe: "Promoting the student affairs profession and extending its knowledge base can be accomplished via contributions to . . . literature (e.g., journals and monographs). Additionally, reading professional literature and using it as a foundation for practice is advisable" (pp. 397–398). However, there may be some disconnect between what we in student affairs say is important when it comes to literature and what we actually do. In the preface to his dissertation on the socialization of master's students to professional values in student affairs, Dan Bureau (2011) writes: "Student affairs literature has talked about learning, assessment, creating partnerships with academic affairs, and connecting people across differences for some time now . . . however, I was hearing master's students talk about . . . planning the best residence hall program or advising Greek Week . . . I was not hearing them articulate the emerging priorities in the literature." Carpenter and Stimpson (2007, p. 272) strike a similar chord when they note,

> . . . there is a lack of systematic and detailed scholarship in the field that follows an agenda from start to wherever it leads, or better, several agendas. And if there were such scholarship available, would practitioners be able to read it, even if they had time to do so? Many would argue the answer is no.

It should not be a surprise coming from colleagues who are themselves active scholars, but we add our voices to those who argue that professional literature be viewed as an important tool in informing professional practice in student affairs. In doing so, we are not simply speaking of being consumers of articles, columns, chapters, monographs, or books, though we certainly believe that reading is fundamental to good practice. We include as a tool for change contributing to the intellectual resources of the field by writing, whether in the more traditional vehicles for publication or in blogs and other vehicles for sharing ideas afforded through technological innovation (see Chapter 4). While not a contribution to the literature in the way that is commonly understood, making presentations at workshops or conferences is nonetheless also an important way to contribute to the shared intellectual assets of the student affairs profession.

Collecting, Understanding, and Using Data

Monitoring perceptions of campus programs, services, or environment. Identifying the needs of students, employers, or some other constituency. Making a formative or summative evaluation of an academic or retention initiative. Measuring student learning. These are all examples of purposes for which data might be collected, but collection alone is unlikely to contribute to desired change.

Paraphrasing Desler (2000), good student affairs work includes understanding data. Data used in student affairs professional practice typically comes from one of two processes: assessment or research. The two are sometimes confused, and the terms are sometimes used interchangeably. However, Erwin (1991) points out there are some important distinctions between assessment and research. "First, assessment guides good practice, while research guides theory and conceptual foundations. Second, assessment typically has implications for a single institution, while research typically has broader implications for student affairs and higher education" (Upcraft and Schuh, 1996, p. 21).

Whatever the purposes, whether the data are a product of assessment or research activities, their full potential in informing and making the case for change is not realized until the data are used to tell the story that needs to be told. Student affairs professionals must purposefully and proactively share the data, whether on campus, in the community, or in professional presentations or publications, if their assessment and research efforts are to make a difference.

One hears a great deal in higher education about data-driven decision making, and one of our points in including discussion about data in this chapter is to recognize data as a tool for addressing challenges and opportunities in student affairs. That said, we argue that decisions should be informed—but not driven—by data. Why? First, there are times when the data might support one decision but our values another. University U, a public institution in South Dakota, might have a need to trim its budget, and as part of its deliberation it might collect data on the number of majors being served, articles produced, or grants received by various departments. They find that Native American studies ranks low on all three measures. Should that department be cut? What about the responsibility of University U to the Native American people in the state (or to all people in the state) to have an academic program focused on an important community in South Dakota? Is the number of articles being produced a fair measure given the challenges of having articles on Native American issues accepted in mainstream journals?

One last point on collecting, understanding, and using data. We agree with Dick McKaig, a student affairs professional and leader for many years, who once observed that just because something cannot be measured does not mean it has no value (McKaig, 2009).

Recognizing and Unpacking Boxes

All of us come to our current work through a collection of personal, educational, and professional experiences. As a result of these experiences we have learned to view our world through a set of assumptions, perceptions, and ways of thinking. In other words, we have an intellectual box. That box provides us both structure and shelter as we move through our daily lives, but it also limits us in some ways. An important exercise is to recognize our box and what it offers us and how it hinders us. If one simply draws on theories, research, and data available to us in our box, we are more likely to perpetuate the status quo than we are to help promote sustained change.

Many of us are socialized in a traditional view of what it means to be a member of a profession—including a credential, privileged knowledge, and privileged language. Our professional box may lead us to overlook the ways in which those who come to student affairs work through other pathways can contribute to change through their knowledge and experience.

Moving beyond the box requires self-awareness—recognizing our own world view and how it is shaped. It also requires knowledge about other ways of seeing the world. The broad array of critical theory can be helpful given that so many are trained in a functionalist tradition, but it is not as simple as functional/critical theory.

Case Studies

The case studies in this section are intended to illustrate ways in which theory, literature, and data might serve as tools for bringing about change in student affairs programs or services. We also encourage colleagues to also consider the recommendations on this subject that are available in the literature of the field (Patton and Harper, 2009).

Urban University

Central City College, a private urban institution, is located in the heart of a large city. Its academic and administrative programs are housed in high-rise buildings. While they do have some attractive commons spaces which are heavily used by students, they do not have campus housing. In recent years the Central City College Student Association (CCCSA), a consistently small but hardworking group of student leaders, has spoken repeatedly with the Director of Campus Life about their interest in improving the sense of belonging amongst students at the college. Several years ago a newly elected group of student leaders made this issue their highest priority for the coming year, and a few weeks later they met with the Director of Campus Life regarding that goal. The Director recognized that, while the students were not familiar with student affairs literature on community or retention, their concerns and comments clearly aligned with models of community and engagement.

The officers opened the meeting by sharing what they saw as the desired goal. They talked about sense of belonging, sense of community, involvement, activity, spirit, and pride. After listening to the leaders, the director of Student Life asked them if they had a sense of how many students shared their perceptions regarding campus life. The CCCSA officers indicated everyone they know felt this way, which prompted the director to invite the student leaders to give some thought to who they are and how that may shape who they know. The director, who has been at CCC for a number of years, indicated the institution was certainly attracted to the same goal but wondered whether they (the institution and the student government) might benefit from collecting some data from students about their thoughts on the matter. Campus Life and CCCSA agreed to co-sponsor a survey project to explore how important, if at all, it is to students at CCC that they have a sense of belonging—a sense of community, involvement, activity, spirit, and pride when it comes to CCC. The survey also asked to what extent, if any, students already felt they had those feelings about CCC. Once the data came back, Campus Life and CCCSA analyzed them to identify challenges and opportunities reflected in them. A presentation was placed on the CCCSA website (with links from several pages for CCC) that presented the findings and invited students to share suggestions for how to move forward on the data.

One finding from the data was a group of students who were highly connected and highly satisfied. In addition, there was also a substantial majority of students who felt some modest sense of connection to the college. However, few in the latter group felt that connection was meeting their needs or wants. Through feed-back from the presentation a number of suggestions were received indicating students had an interest in exploring the artistic, cultural, and entertainment options in the city as part of a CCC group. The director recalled having read about the work of Martínez Alemán and Wartman (2009), which indicated students seemed more likely to use social media to extend community rather than create it. That information was shared with the CCSA leaders. They recognized that social media might be a way to engage the base of students who felt at least some sense of connection but who wanted to participate more in activities. The leaders decided to host a series of Tweet up events (social gathering organized using Twitter) for students at local art galleries, museums, and coffee houses. Those who attended were invited to suggest other locations where Tweet ups might be held.

As the end of the academic year approached, CCCSA and Campus Life used email to contact the students who had partici-pated in the Tweet ups and asked them to respond to a few open-ended questions about their experiences at those events and since those events, with the understanding that their comments sans individual identification might be used in reporting and marketing for the program. The qualitative data indicated that participants were happy to have the opportunity to meet fellow CCC students with similar interests in a semi-structured environment that did not require a major commitment of their time or resources. There were a number of comments about people following up with those they met to take part in additional events around the city or simply to share a conversation in one of the campus commons. There were also a number of comments indicating participants felt a stronger sense of community as a result of the program. The plan is to use these testimonials, without individual identifiers and with permission, as part of the promotion of the Tweet up program moving forward.

Discussion. Adapting a theory for use in the unique context of an institution may be far more fruitful than strictly adhering to that theory. The same is certainly true when considering models of practice or ways of understanding gleaned from professional literature or data from research, and assessment by its very definition is a local enterprise. The director of Student Life at CCC recognized that the students' concerns and comments reflected the informal theories they were using in considering the quality of campus life, and the Director purposefully connected those informal theories to formal theory informing student affairs professional practice.

With regard to adapting theory or making use of informal theories, what Argyris and Schön (1974) called theories in use, we encourage readers to review a recent discussion regarding the use of theory in student affairs practice. In that discussion, Love (2012) makes an argument for theories in use as a primary vehicle through which professional practice is and ought to be enacted, and Evans and Guido (2012) offer a counterargument that formal theory is better suited for that purpose given the rigor with which it is developed and tested. While not denying that theories in use are prevalent in professional practice, Evans and Guido suggest that if they are brought to bear they ought to be premised on formal theory.

The phrase "all politics is local" is typically attributed to Tip O'Neill, a former Speaker of the United States House of Representatives (O'Neill, 1995). It is our observation that the best uses of theory, literature, and data are too. This case study helps illustrate that point. The director of student life adapted formal theory to the local urban setting of CCC and to work with a widely diverse student body. Further, the director collected data to help understand local construction of notions of community and engagement. Finally, the director creatively connected more traditional theoretical work regarding community and engagement with emerging scholarship related to students' use of computer-mediated communication and social media (addressed in Chapter 4) to help students develop a program uniquely tailored for CCC students.

Southwestern Desert State

The dean of students at Southwestern Desert State (SDS) received a report that one of the fraternities on campus had engaged in some vandalism to the property of another fraternity during the run up to the campus' annual celebration of Greek life at SDS. Acts such as this were not unheard of at SDS, and the fraternity that allegedly participated in the vandalism was a group that had frequently been invited to meet with the dean regarding various other incidents.

This year, however, the dean had been presented with a unique opportunity. Last year the student who had become president of the fraternity in question was an upperclassmen who had taken a leadership course taught by the dean and had also had the chance to interact with the dean in a committee exploring ways to incorporate ethics and values development into programs and services being offered at SDS. This led to the dean's being invited to present at a workshop earlier this year that the fraternity president had organized for Interfraternity Council on ethical leadership. At that workshop the dean had introduced the student leaders to the work of Kohlberg (1958, 1971) on moral development as way of understanding how they and their peers might be developing as people and as leaders.

The dean sent a message to the fraternity president inviting him to come in to talk about the alleged behavior. During that meeting the fraternity president privately acknowledged that the vandalism had taken place, and there was a division within the fraternity about how to handle what had occurred. Some were frustrated that their brothers had poorly represented their group. Others were puzzled that anything was being made of the matter just because they were caught doing what others did without getting in trouble. Yet another group spoke with pride about being a brave and tough enough bunch to have put together such a clever and daring raid on a rival. The fraternity president seemed puzzled and frustrated by how the conversation was playing out among his brothers, and asked the dean for a few days to come up with a plan for the house to deal appropriately with what happened. The dean agreed.

Two days later there as a knock at the dean's door, and the fraternity president entered. He had a smile on his face and a proposal in his hand. He sat at the desk and exclaimed, "I get it. Some of them are Stage 1, 2, or 3. I'm a 5. Here's our plan for working with all of them." After reviewing the plan, it was the dean's turn to smile.

Discussion. The dean of students at Southwestern Desert State's handling of this case demonstrates an important point. Knowledge of theory (and literature and data for that matter) does not belong to student affairs. That knowledge ought to be available to our students, staff, and faculty colleagues too. Change is more likely to come about when such knowledge is shared so as to engage and inform others who can help bring about the desired outcomes rather than when such knowledge is hidden or hoarded. In this case, the dean shares knowledge of theory in group settings (the course, committee, and workshop) and through conversations with the fraternity president.

We Are All in the Circle

A number of years ago a group of Native American and non-Native scholars and practitioners published a monograph on serving and supporting Native American students (Fox, Lowe, and McClellan, 2005). This work, which at the time was one-of-a-kind, caught the attention of Native American student affairs professionals and others interested in the success of Native American students in higher education.

Conversations and presentations related to the monograph helped bring more individuals together—some from existing professional organizations and others who had been working on their own in various higher education settings. The informal group began to serve as advocates for issues related to the success of Native American students and student affairs practitioners. They worked to educate student affairs professionals and others regarding Native

American students and about how to work respectfully with tribal communities. Members of the group encouraged Native American graduate students in master's and doctoral programs in student affairs and higher education to complete their degree work and offered support related to proposing and writing theses or dissertations on issues related to Native Americans in higher education. Working within the framework of a larger existing professional association, the group organized, identified funding for, and presented a national conference on Native American student success.

In addition to their efforts with the conference, the group regularly shared emerging literature and research on Native American issues. They actively lobbied the professional journals and publishers to be intentional about including work on Native Americans in their publications. They began work to develop a formal professional association to support the success of Native American students and student affairs professionals. Recently, members of the group edited a hardbound volume on serving Native American students in higher education (Shotton, Lowe, and Waterman, 2013)—completing the circle that was first formed to discuss the monograph published eight years earlier.

Discussion. The colleagues in this study recognized that the prevailing construction of the practice of student affairs and much of the theory, research, and data associated with that professional practice reflects realities not aligned with those of many Native American people in higher education or ignores those people all together. They set about to bring about change that would have a positive impact on Native American people in higher education (particularly students), on their own professional practice, and on the student affairs profession as a whole. As a result of their activities, the members of the group (both Native and non-Native) became more aware of an Indigenous model for student affairs practice as a result of their journey together. They have also helped shape important change in the profession by helping others see beyond their own boxes.

Spiritual University

Like many universities around the country, Spiritual University (SU), a mid-sized religiously affiliated university in the Pacific northwest, was concerned about improving its retention and graduation rates. The vice president for enrollment management had been working with the Enrollment Management Advisory Committee to develop a strategic plan for retention, and as part of their work the group had been reviewing their institutional data.

The members of the committee were struck by the relatively large disparity between retention and graduation rates for women and men. Despite what some acknowledged as assumptions they held about the success of male students in college, it was clear from SU's data that the disparity extended across ethnicities, ages, and disciplines. The vice president formed a subcommittee to explore the available literature and data regarding male retention and graduation rates at peer institutions, similar institutions, and across the country (Davis, 2013). The subcommittee reported that the literature and available databases indicated similar disparities at other institutions, but it appeared that SU's performance in this area did lag behind that of similar institutions.

The vice president and members of the committee decided the data, analysis, and findings ought to be shared with campus leadership, including students, staff, and faculty. They scheduled a day-long workshop during which a national expert on the success of men in college shared national data, information on the implications and impact of the data, and several theories and models of practice that might be used in understanding and addressing the phenomenon. The vice president then presented SU's local data and invited participants to respond to it. A member of the faculty noted that their experience had been that the male students who leave do so much earlier than the female students who leave. After the workshop, the vice president ran the data on male student departure at SU and confirmed the faculty member's observation. A much greater proportion of male student departure occurred within the first semester than was the case for female departures.

SU had an online program that invites students to share how they are adjusting to college in their first several weeks and months on campus. The vice president asked the coordinator of that program to pull the data from the males who left in the first semester for the past three years. Several factors emerged as potential threats to freshmen male persistence, but one in particular that stood out was students' perceptions regarding their coursework as being isolating. There was a clearly expressed interest in having more opportunities to work with other students in groups as opposed to working alone. There was also a strong indication that some of the men are having trouble finding connections between their coursework and their interests or plans for the future.

The vice chancellor took the findings to the Academic Leadership Council, a group that included the deans and department chairs. Together they decided to work with faculty members teaching gateway courses that were part of the general education curriculum to incorporate more teamwork and to more explicitly connect content to career and personal interests. An assessment plan was put in place to follow up on what impact, if any, the changes had on the retention of male students at SU. The campus awaits the results.

Discussion. It is likely to be the case that fostering programs and services to address challenges and opportunities will be a collaborative effort involving a diverse array of partners and participants. The leaders involved in the case at Spiritual University were explicit and transparent with all involved, including with students themselves, regarding theory, literature, or data that in some way informed the leaders' perspectives. This proved helpful in several ways. First, it fostered a shared understanding of the issue at hand. Second, it stimulated new ideas and new ways of thinking, which improved the effort. Finally, it allowed the opportunity for others to serve as reviewers—offering critique as a means of strengthening the program together.

Conclusion

In their classic article on the ways in which organizational fields structure themselves, DiMaggio and Powell (1983) note that in the face of uncertain circumstances organizations tend to take on the shape of other, like organizations facing similar conditions—a phenomenon they described as mimetic isomorphism. Put more simply, when in doubt as to what success can or should look like, organizations tend to make themselves look like their peer organizations.

DiMaggio and Powell (1983) point to cosmopolitan professionals (those moving between organizations) and consultants as two entities playing a primary role in this process. We believe misunderstanding or misuse of theory, literature, and data can also contribute to mimetic isomorphism. These tools are best used to inform the pursuit of success rather than how success is defined.

Imagine relying only on the resources of the past when giving thought to helping students explore the ways in which their use of social media impacts on their sense of community. Can one really reframe their student affairs practice as an educational enterprise (see Chapter 6) without having at least passing familiarity with recent theory, literature, and data regarding neuroplasticity? Wouldn't it be unfortunate if a new professional struggling with how to integrate theory into his or her practice was to be unaware of Reason and Kimball's (2012) thoughtful and promising new model for doing just that?

Those working in student affairs put in a great number of hours supporting the students and institutions they serve, and some do so while continuing to pursue additional educational goals. Coupled with commitments to the joys and responsibilities of everyday life, student affairs professionals are on the whole a very busy group of people. As noted earlier, many feel they do not have time to stay current on theory, literature, and data. That feeling will not change unless staying current is internalized by practitioners as being essential to successfully supporting the success of students and institutions, but internalization of this perspective will not fully address the time constraints faced by student affairs professionals. It is also important that one develop strategies for quickly and effectively reviewing new literature. Focus efforts on environments rich in information where many, if not most, of what is shared is relevant to your work or interests. Even in such rich environments, scan the material and read selectively. Develop a network of colleagues who, like you, are interested in staying current and create a habit of sharing interesting work with one another. Finally, accept and respect your own decisions with regard to when you can focus on staying current and when you cannot. It is realistic that you will get some reading done; it is not realistic that you will read everything.

With regard to assessment, there is a great deal of attention given to measuring progress toward outcomes and the impact, if any, of programs and services on outcomes. There is no doubt that assessment of outcomes is important and it is an obligation of professional practice in student affairs. However, we in student affairs understand that the story of the journey is more than just the destination. It is also about why you started and how you got there. Assessing purpose and process can be very instructive. What do our goals or our vision say about who we are? How do people experience the way in which the campus goes about pursuing its goals? Like questions about outcomes, these are questions worth asking in the course of addressing challenges and opportunities.

In writing about the future of professional practice in student affairs, McClellan and Stringer (2009) observe,

> One way to assure the continued vitality of student affairs is to recommit ourselves to the scholarly practice of our profession. This includes engaging in conventional forms of scholarship as well as the scholarship of practice. Simply put, we must seek to better understand

our students, our institutions, our contexts, and the complex interactions between them. We must then share those understandings through presentation and publication, subjecting our findings to the scrutiny of others while sharing our newfound knowledge. (p. 633)

We echo their observation and note that utilizing and contributing to theory, literature, and data are scholarly acts of practice in student affairs, but they may not necessarily help foster change. They may, in fact, reinforce the status quo. The difference between these two possibilities is the spirit with which the work is approached.

Reflective Questions

1. What is your assessment of your knowledge of theory, literature, and data that relate to your professional practice?

2. What is your assessment of the extent to which you have made conscious efforts to use your knowledge of theory, literature, and data in your professional practice?

3. What do you see as the culture of your department, division, and institution when it comes to explicitly drawing on theory, literature, or data in addressing a challenge or opportunity?

4. Can you identify an instance when you attempted to make use of theory, literature, or data to bring about a change on your campus? How was that effort received? What was the result of the effort? If you are unable to identify such an instance, why is that the case?

5. What strategies might you pursue to help strengthen the culture of your department, division, and institution with regard to using theory, literature, or data to help bring about desired change?

3

Using Resources to Effect Change

S tudent affairs administrators have many resources available to
them in their efforts to improve student learning. Among these
resources are money, facilities, the community, faculty, students,
and of course, their own staff. The purpose of this chapter is to
demonstrate how student affairs leaders can serve as change agents
in the use of resources. It is no longer sufficient merely to manage
resources; student affairs leaders are now expected to make positive
improvements in services, facilities, and educational programs by
using available resources and by securing additional resources.
Student affairs administrators need to be experts in identifying
needs and problems, and also in finding resources and using these
resources effectively to improve student learning.

This chapter discusses some significant challenges faced in
securing and using resources and describes briefly selected insights
from the organizational change literature useful to student affairs
leaders. It also discusses strategies in identifying, securing, and using
resources in conjunction with institutional case studies that illustrate how student affairs leaders can use resources effectively to
make positive change happen. Learning how to become effective
change agents by wisely using resources is important to achieving
success in student affairs administration.

Challenges in Securing and Using Resources

Student affairs administrators are committed to improving the education of students and know that to accomplish their goals, they need resources. The following is a brief description of some of the significant challenges they are now facing and will likely face in the future.

Diminished Institutional Funds

Since the economic recession of 2008, both public and private colleges and universities have had to face serious budgetary short-falls. Funding from state legislatures has decreased in actual dollars for public institutions, and many private colleges have seen the value of their endowments decrease during the past five years (*Chronicle of Higher Education*, 2012). This has often resulted in substantial increases in tuition to meet institutional needs, and in some cases, the elimination of certain academic programs and cutbacks in faculty and staff. Some student affairs programs and staff have had to be reduced or discontinued and proposals for needed new programs have had to be set aside. This economic situation for higher education has made it more difficult for student affairs leaders to accomplish their goals and has often caused them to be less dependent upon institutional funds. It has also forced them to seek additional resources in new and creative ways.

Increased Demands for Services and Programs

Despite the economic recession since 2008, the expectations for more extensive services for students continue to increase. These demands are coming from the students themselves, from the parents of students, and from the general society. This is particularly true in campus safety and mental health services. The tragic shooting deaths at Virginia Tech, Northern Illinois, Iowa, and other institutions in the past few years have made it clear that the public expects substantially more police protection, safety and security measures, and mental health education and support for students, faculty, and staff. Moreover, the competition among colleges and universities themselves to attract and retain students has led to more facilities— the construction of expensive new residence halls, recreation centers, and student unions. This has placed increased pressure on student affairs leaders to find the resources that can enable their institutions to provide the expected services, staff, and facilities.

Increased Public Visibility and Scrutiny

Colleges and universities are no longer isolated enclaves whose activities are unknown to or of little concern to the general public. With almost 20 million students attending some 4500 higher education institutions (*Chronicle of Higher Education*, 2012), and with student debt a national political issue, higher education is frequently in the news. The significant numbers of college graduates unable to find jobs, coupled with tuition increases that have often outstripped the rate of inflation, have exacerbated this situation. This has resulted in public debates about such matters as the content of the curriculum, the alleged worth of certain academic courses, and the need for various programs, services, and facilities. Student affairs leaders may be asked to justify the content and purposes of some of their programs by members of the public who object to them on political or religious grounds. At the same time, these student affairs leaders may be chastised for not providing more support and services in areas certain members of the public deem important, such as campus security and mental health services. In their efforts to find resources to accomplish their goals and to use these resources to improve educational services, student affairs leaders now recognize that the ivy walls afford them little protection from a public that is subjecting them to much more scrutiny.

Changing Patterns of Institutional Governance

On many campuses, administrative leaders feel increasingly on their own as competition for resources among academic units increases.

The principle of responsibility-centered management budgeting has become more common in the past few years, as governing boards, presidents, and provosts strive to make their institutions more accountable and to use their available resources in the most efficient manner. This can cause some individual academic units to feel as if their only alternative is to act alone, in their own best interests, without much regard for the campus as a whole. Diminished cooperation and collaboration between and among academic units and with administrative divisions is often the result. This approach may have some advantages for major academic units with extensive, external resources, but it can be devastating to other, less privileged units. For student affairs leaders this situation poses a major challenge, as their effectiveness as leaders depends more than ever on collaboration and cooperation with all aspects of the institution.

Myths About How Change Occurs

Among the necessary realities for student affairs leaders to learn is a realistic understanding of how change occurs within institutions. While organizational change has been the focus of thousands of studies and books for decades, there is little agreement among scholars or practitioners about the best way to achieve change. However, there are some myths about change in higher education that, if viewed as fact by student affairs leaders, can seriously hinder their efforts to secure and use resources to advance student learning. One of the myths sometimes assumed as fact within student affairs itself is that data will drive decision making and, in itself, will convince others of the worth of a proposal. Another is that top-down decision making, as opposed to a more participative, democratic model, will simply go away. Yet another is that cooperation and building relationships with others will surely result in the good will of institutional decision makers and will convince them to provide resources for student affairs. This is not to suggest that student affairs leaders should abandon their traditional commitments to such values; it is an admonition to them not to be naïve in their efforts to secure and use resources. If they choose to act in accordance with these myths about how change actually takes place, it is unlikely that they will achieve much success. They must become strong and savvy leaders, advocating effectively for their programs and policies in campus and community settings where the competition is rigorous. The case studies presented later in this chapter provide illustrations of how student affairs administrators can become change-oriented leaders.

Changing Students

Scholars and the general public never seem to tire in their willingness to assign the latest generation of students a new label. But as any good student affairs professional knows, none of the dozens of student labels assigned to students over the years does justice to the richness and diversity of the 20 million students in American higher education. Nonetheless, there seems to be general agreement that students entering colleges and universities in 2014 present special challenges, and that it is very important for institutions to strive to understand the lives and needs of these new students. Three brief, recent studies provide evidence for concern: Arum and Roksa's (2011) study described academically adrift students, who evidenced little improvement in critical thinking while in college and showed a sharp decline in both academic work effort and learning. Levine and Dean (2012) describe a generation on a tightrope, suggesting that students are often uncomfortable with face-to-face communication but quite adept at digital skills. The authors also argue that current colleges and universities must change their educational programs to adapt to these new students. Kuh and his associates (2011), in their use of the National Study of Student Engagement at many institutions, have described the wide variation in the quality of the undergraduate experience, the level of academic challenge, and the frequency of student-faculty interactions. The best student affairs administrators have always been sensitive to changing students and to the needs of students often missed or ignored by others.

The challenge now, as in earlier years, is to understand the real experiences of the students entering higher education and to devise effective service and support programs for them. This will require significantly more resources, and student affairs leaders are responsible for making this happen.

Online Instruction and Services

As advances in technology continue to occur, online instruction and services, already common, will certainly increase. The introduction of free Massive, Open, Online Courses (MOOCs) in 2012 resulted in a great deal of attention being given to new private, non-profit delivery systems, such as Coursera, Udacity, and edX (Pappano, 2012). Many prestigious universities quickly partnered with these companies, or started similar programs of their own. There are already more than a million students signed up for such courses and widespread speculation about what this might all mean for traditional credits, tuition, and accreditation. Whatever direction this movement takes, it is clear that student affairs administrators face significant challenges in providing effective online services to students. Services such as registration, academic advising, financial aid, career placement, and personal counseling need to be provided. Most student affairs programs, of course, have been focused on a traditional campus with face-to-face contact with resident students. As significantly more students take courses and earn degrees online, student affairs leaders will need to rethink and redesign what they do with these students, and especially, how to deliver the services. This will require new resources, which will take special efforts to secure and to use wisely.

Of course, there are other challenges in higher education and student affairs (for example, staff development, international education, diversity) for which student affairs leaders will need to secure additional resources to improve student learning. Moreover, in this fast-paced world of change, some of the challenges are currently unknown. What is clear is that student affairs administrators need to understand the major challenges in securing and using resources and be aggressive in their efforts to respond with effective programs and services. It is their responsibility to acquire new resources and, especially, to use them for the benefit of their students.

Applying Insights from Organizational Change Literature

The literature on organizational change is vast and while much of the research has been conducted with corporations and businesses, student affairs leaders can learn valuable insights from the thousands of studies done on change. The theme of this book is that it is the responsibility of student affairs administrators to assume a leadership role in change—in order to, enhance student learning. The extensive literature on organizational change represents a treasure trove for student affairs leaders (Kuh, 2003), and the following selections represent authors whose insights are especially applicable to student affairs.

In reviewing over a hundred organization change studies, Kotter (2008, p. vii) found that more than 70 percent of the change efforts in these organizations failed. However, about 10 percent of them succeeded, and these organizations had several characteristics in common. Among these were a sense of urgency transmitted by the leader, a supportive culture, and a long-term commitment to life-long learning for the members of the organization (Kotter and Cohen, 2002, pp. 3–6). Student affairs administrators sometimes may be hesitant to initiate changes because they fear they may not be successful. It is difficult to know if change efforts will succeed, but as Kotter (1996, p. 117) argues, by creating "short term wins that nourish faith in the change effort," good momentum toward the eventual goal can occur. In their efforts to secure and use resources, student affairs administrators should carefully consider these researchers' insights. They need to distinguish between management and leadership, acknowledging that managers may focus mainly on planning and controlling, while leaders focus on motivating, inspiring, and establishing direction. Student affairs administrators should select and carefully consider the changes they want to initiate, while also paying close attention to timing. But they will always have to deal with obstacles; if they think they cannot act until all the obstacles go away, it is likely they will do nothing.

James O'Toole is among the most influential authorities on organizational change, and in *Leading Change* (1995, p. 14) he suggests ways to "overcome the ideology of comfort and the tyranny of custom." He rejects contingency or situational theory, which suggests that leaders do whatever the circumstances require. This approach, according to O'Toole, results in inconsistent behavior in leaders and most important, a diminution of trust. His leadership model argues for listening to people in the organization and respecting them because the welfare of these people is the end of leadership. What creates trust is the leader's respect for the members of the organization. In discussing successful efforts to produce change in organizations, O'Toole (1995, p. 11) emphasizes that leaders themselves have to go beyond the intellectual commitment to the change—they must demonstrate to others that their hearts are in it, with integrity and vision. Moreover, if leaders resort to manipulation of others to achieve their goals, they will lose the trust that is essential for change to happen. Student affairs leaders have to do more than simply acquire and manage resources. They need to build trust on and off the campus, and demonstrate a sincere, consistent passion for the benefits of what they are proposing. If they can honestly convince students, faculty, administrators, and their own staff that additional resources are needed and can result in positive new educational opportunities when used effectively, they will enhance their chances of achieving successful change. Student affairs administrators committed to change—improving learning opportunities for their students, enhancing facilities and programs, and making their campuses more inclusive—should pay close attention to O'Toole's work. With patience and passion for their work, student affairs administrators can build trust with others and demonstrate their ability to lead.

Edgar Schein's (2010) work on organizational culture for many years has stimulated leaders to think carefully about group and interpersonal relationships in their efforts to initiate change. Schein demonstrated that organizations evolve through stages, and in order for leaders to be effective, they must not only understand the differences between young, midlife, and mature organizational cultures, but also pay close attention to timing. Some change strategies, Schein argued, are more likely to succeed when an organization is in its early growth period than when it is in its mature stage. For example, a major change in admissions policy may only be possible if it is introduced when the culture of the institution is mature enough to consider it seriously. Student affairs administrators need to understand the specific culture of their institutions, and not assume that what and how they initiated change in a previous institution might work in their current institution. The process they use to find and use new resources may depend upon the institution's traditions, the community in which it is located, how open the culture is to new ideas, and the history of how student affairs administrators are perceived on the campus. The culture of the campus may not be used to seeing student affairs administrators initiate change by seeking and acquiring new resources. While campus cultures are powerful and must be understood, they are not permanently static, and good leaders can challenge some of the traditional ways that change has been pursued in the past. William R. Butler, a successful senior student affairs administrator who spent more than 30 years in his position at the University of Miami, indicated that what was going on in the community, in the country, and on the campus at a given time drove how he went about initiating changes (Sandeen, 2001, p. 61).

Among the most widely used leadership practices are those advanced by James Kouzes and Barry Posner (2012) as a result of their extensive work and study for many years with organizations.

Their five fundamental practices to make change happen emerged from their observation of successful leaders: challenge the process, inspire a shared vision, enable others to act, model the way, and encourage the heart. They found successful leaders to be those who venture out, challenging assumptions about what the organization can and should be, and inspiring others to act mainly by setting an example and demonstrating to members of the organization that they are appreciated and valued. Student affairs leaders intent on finding and using resources cannot succeed in this task without becoming visible, passionate, and credible (Kouzes and Posner, 2011) on the campus and in the community for their commitment to student learning and welfare. This will require a great deal of energy and a willingness to demonstrate strength when others may respond with criticism or obstruction. These authors argue for leaders to demonstrate courage and to advocate vigorously for the changes they are seeking. If student affairs leaders are to become successful in the acquisition and effective application of new resources, they will do well to heed the insights of these authors.

Some student affairs administrators may relish the public forum and may flourish in the open and often raucous debates that are necessary to be successful in their change efforts. This not only requires courage and self-confidence; it also requires leaders who can deal with public criticism and stress. Very few student affairs administrators develop such skills quickly in their careers—they are learned over many years, and only by those willing to take the risks.

Peter Senge's (2006) advocacy for a learning organization and Robert Greenleaf's (2012) concept of servant leadership offer additional valuable insights for student affairs leaders. When members of an organization believe that the organization genuinely is committed to their learning, and when these members are, in fact, active participants in this learning, the entire enterprise can thrive. Conversely, if the members' ideas are not listened to or are viewed as unimportant, the organization itself is unlikely to progress.

Organizations, like individuals, need to continue to learn in order to grow and succeed. The leader as servant is especially relevant to student affairs administrators, whose primary charge is to improve the education of students. Listening to students and others and reaching out to those who have not been well served (or even noticed) by the institution can enable student affairs administrators to become trusted advocates (servants) and effective agents of change. To serve the institution most effectively, student affairs administrators should learn to listen carefully to the needs being expressed on and off campus, and in so doing, build credibility and trust, which will enable them to find and use resources more effectively.

The challenges of acquiring and using resources are often daunting, and the process requires student affairs administrators who are strong, persistent, passionate, and courageous. The insights gained from the organizational change literature provide a valuable resource for student affairs administrators who want to initiate change and make it happen. The education of students is at stake, and thus, the efforts are well worth making.

Case Studies

This section describes five student affairs issues at various colleges and universities that require more resources and the effective use of these resources to make positive change happen. The five issues are a new bus system, academic advising, improvements in mental health services, a new union-recreation facility, and a new student affairs development office. The strategies and actions of student affairs leaders to acquire and use needed resources at these institutions are also described. The cases are illustrative of how change can occur.

A New Bus System at Alpha University

Alpha is a large, public university located in a city of 125,000 people. Almost all of the students are full time, and there are extensive graduate and professional school programs. Of the 48,000 students, about 7500 live on campus, while the rest live in private apartments within three to five miles of the campus. For many years, Alpha had a contract with the county's regional bus system, which provided bus service to the campus from the surrounding community and within the campus itself. Funds for this contract came from Alpha's general fund, and were the subject of annual negotiations with the county administration. The regional bus system itself lost money each year, and was the object of considerable criticism in the city and on the campus. Students, staff, and faculty had little trust in the bus system, as the buses were often in poor condition and the service was undependable. As a result, ridership declined each year, and students balked at the required 50 cents per ride.

While the business vice president had responsibility for the bus system at Alpha, the new student affairs vice president decided that she should try to do something about this perennial problem. In the five months she had been in her job, she had become very visible on the campus and in the community, meeting directly with students, faculty, administrators, city and county elected officials, and business leaders. A good listener, she heard many people complain about the poorly functioning bus system. Rather than blaming the problem on anyone, she decided to research it on her own, and was not surprised to learn that the regional bus system was so poorly funded that it had little chance of ever improving its service. In the next 18 months, she worked closely with her business affairs vice president, the city manager, the mayor, and Alpha's student government leaders to form a joint Alpha-City-County task force to study the bus system and suggest solutions to improve it. During this time, she visited directly with the task force, shared information from other campuses that had successful bus systems, and joined with the task force in visiting a similar campus in a nearby state, where a model university-city bus system was operating. She also continued to have several one-on-one meetings with key individuals involved in this matter, and explored various options with them about ways to generate sufficient resources to establish a successful bus system. She knew Alpha itself could not substantially increase its subsidy of the bus system from its institutional budget, which had again been reduced by the state legislature. But she remained determined to move forward, expressing optimism and enthusiasm for an improved system. In the process, she gained a reputation as someone who genuinely cared about good services and as someone who worked very hard to accomplish a goal.

During the task force's work on the bus system, the student affairs vice president began discussions with student government leaders about the possibility of a special student transportation fee that would guarantee sufficient funding for the bus system, and at the same time enable registered students to ride the buses free of charge. Key student government officers, after some weeks of debate and discussion, realized that their support of such a fee might enshrine them as outstanding leaders in the long history of student government at Alpha! The student affairs vice president then arranged several meetings with the business vice president, the director of the regional bus system, the student government president, and the mayor to discuss the specifics of an earmarked, student transportation fee. She already had cleared all this with her president, who was hopeful but skeptical about this project. Student government leaders knew that the institution of such a fee would require a campus referendum and they took the lead in preparing for this, and they immediately began campaigning for its adoption.

After three years of seeking a change that was not part of her own administrative portfolio, the student affairs vice president was very pleased when the students enthusiastically voted to support the bus system with the new transportation fee. Now, some four years later, the bus system is profitable and is operating very efficiently. Best of all, according to the student affairs vice president, the current students and faculty take it for granted as a service they can depend upon, and the student government association at Alpha continues to get the credit for its success.

Discussion. The student affairs vice president's strategy was to show persistence, patience, an ability to listen, and the skill to engage a broad array of constituents in the effort. In the end, her determination, the trust and respect she built, and her organization skills proved successful. She was also very pleased that those she involved so extensively in the process took responsibility for the change! She could have chosen to ignore this issue on her campus, believing that a bus system is someone else's responsibility and that this is really not a core educational issue. But she viewed herself as a campus leader and was confident in her ability to improve an important service, and she did it!

Academic Advising at Beta College

Beta College is a regional state-supported institution of 16,000 students. Most of the students live close to campus, and the most popular academic majors are education, psychology, and business administration. Beta is not very selective in its admissions, but it enjoys a mostly positive reputation in this midwestern state, and its faculty are stable and quite traditional. Students are required to complete a general education core in their first two years, which comprises about half of their academic program, and then must select their academic major by the end of their second year.

The dean of students at Beta, the senior student affairs officer, had been in his position for two years, having come from another, similar institution. He earned a good reputation for his concern for students, his positive relations with the faculty, and his willingness to work hard. But he was increasingly disturbed about the fact that most Beta students took five years to graduate and also about their persistent complaints about not being able to enroll for various courses needed in their academic majors. Moreover, since he had been at Beta, he often listened to angry parents of students, who complained that they were fed up with hearing tales of woe from their sons and daughters, who don't seem to get any help in getting their courses. The dean of students discussed this issue with the provost and with individual faculty members, but they responded by placing the blame on the students themselves, for not knowing what they want to do and for procrastination.

Students were assigned to specific faculty for academic advising at Beta College. However, such advising was not a high priority for many faculty, and some students barely knew or met with their faculty adviser, especially since they could sign up for their classes online after reading what the requirements were for their majors. Student academic progress was not monitored to help assure they would graduate in four years, and there seemed to be little concern among faculty that they did. The dean of students believed the institution could do better and wanted to contribute to a solution to this problem.

The dean was responsible for the Career Development Center, one of the units within his student affairs division. The center's role is to provide support and counseling to students about their careers, but it had little contact with faculty and was mainly visited by students when they were within a semester of graduating and eager to find a job.

Due to decreased financial support from the state legislature, Beta College was facing budget problems, so the dean knew obtaining new faculty or staff positions was highly unlikely. After several meetings he arranged with the provost, key faculty members, and his own staff, the dean made a bold proposal, knowing that it would challenge some of the traditional values of Beta's institutional culture. He suggested that for the first two years of study at Beta, when students' academic programs focus on general education courses, that they be assigned academic advisers in a renamed and refocused Career Advising and Development Center, jointly responsible to him and to the provost. In order to staff this function with full-time advisers, the dean reassigned four lines from his financially successful housing auxiliary and the provost recruited six faculty from the general education program who were close to retirement but interested in serving as full-time advisers. The dean and the provost worked together closely on this plan, knowing that the faculty senate might object to this taking away of one of their traditional responsibilities. But because the dean and the provost explained their actions in detail and listened carefully to their concerns, the faculty senate approved the proposal.

The dean shared and discussed with the provost a model from his previous institution that required students to stay on track in their academic programs, monitoring their course loads, and also guaranteeing students that they will be able to enroll for the courses they need for graduation. The provost was enthusiastic about this model and in conversations with her staff and the other senior administrators at Beta, was assured that it could be implemented with no increase in costs. By the next fall semester, this system was in place, and after two or three years of operation, complaints about the lack of advising by students and parents decreased significantly, and many more students were on track to graduate in four years.

Discussion. The dean of students at Beta takes no credit for this change, but his cooperation with many others, his ability to listen, his persistence, and his optimistic attitude that a solution could be found earned him the respect and admiration of his colleagues. Most important, his strategy was to identify the problem, collaborate with the provost and his own staff to find resources to address it, and work with others to provide improved services to students. Edgar Schein and James O'Toole would have been proud of his leadership efforts!

Need for More Mental Health Services at Gamma University

Gamma University is a large, prestigious public research institution located in a large city in the Southwest. Its enrollment of 42,000 students includes 15,000 graduate and professional school students. The student affairs vice chancellor has an extensive administrative portfolio, which includes the student health service and the counseling center. Gamma is very selective and the academic pressure is intense.

The counseling center staff was overwhelmed with the demand for its services and very concerned with the serious nature of many of the cases brought to its attention. There were twenty-four full-time licensed counseling psychologists in the center, as well as two psychiatrists. The center had a very good reputation on campus, and faculty and staff frequently referred students to it. The student affairs vice chancellor had recently been able to add two full-time positions to the center in response to increased demand, but with nationwide concern for safety and with increased awareness of mental health issues, the need for more counseling services was critical. The vice chancellor was well aware of the problem and also knew that in view of the serious economic downturn in the state, she was very unlikely to secure additional state support for new positions. It was the most serious problem she had faced so far at the institution, as the health and safety of students were at stake.

The vice chancellor for student affairs had shared this problem with her president, the provost, college deans, the faculty senate, and student leaders. While she was received with understanding and concern, she knew that if this issue of providing more mental health services was going to be solved, it would be up to her. The student health service at Gamma was supported by a required student fee, which supported a large facility and staff, including fourteen full-time physicians. The counseling service was funded through the general university budget. There were eleven academic colleges at Gamma, including law and medicine. The student affairs staff worked closely with these colleges and, in three of them, had jointly funded counseling psychologists with offices in their facilities. The demand for more mental health services was especially strong from graduate and professional school students, and from their spouses.

The vice chancellor and her staff knew what the problem was— what they needed was more resources. She decided to form an action team to assist her in this process. She did not expect this team to study the problem; it was tasked with identifying various alternatives to providing more mental health services. She was aware of what some similar institutions were doing to meet such needs, and she shared that information with the action team. She chaired this relatively small team, which consisted of a faculty member, the student government president, a counseling center psychologist, the associate vice chancellor for business affairs, the associate provost, a member of the community-campus religious advisers association, a psychiatrist from the leading community hospital, and a staff member from the development office. She shared her sense of urgency with the team, indicating that she expected action within three months. Rather than simply passing on the problem to the team, she actively and regularly met with them and shared with them various ideas and proposals.

This action team not only proved to be an effective way to generate ideas, it also was a forum that attracted a good deal of discussion and awareness on the entire campus. After considering several alternatives, the vice chancellor, with the support of the action team, was successful in turning over to the institution one-half of the state-supported dollars that funded the counseling center in return for permission to increase the required student health service fee (to be renamed the student health and wellness fee). Within a period of five years, this fee would increase to the point where the counseling center would receive its entire financial support from the fee. She was successful in convincing student government leaders that this fee increase would be less than $80 per student per year. At the same time, she was successful in convincing the Gamma University development office to become more assertive in seeking funds specifically directed toward student mental health services. Some of the most successful fundraising at the institution has since come from grateful former patients in the university's research hospital, and the development staff is optimistic that donors can become similarly interested in supporting mental health. Finally, the student affairs vice chancellor was pleased to support an offer from the thirty-member campus-community

religious advisers association to provide additional counseling services in their facilities, in a cooperative, counseling center supervised program.

Discussion. The student affairs vice chancellor understood the
problem, was sensitive to the realistic ways change can occur in her
institution's culture, demonstrated a sense of urgency in pursuing
the change, and involved key people from important constituencies
in her efforts to secure and use the needed resources. In this carefully
considered change strategy, she tackled the problem by involving
many others, gaining their support and understanding, and moving
ahead, clearly knowing that what she was seeking could fail. But she
was willing to take the risk, and in the process, she learned she had
to be patient. In the end, she solidified her own reputation at
Gamma University as a respected and able leader who was effective
in bring about a positive change.

A New Recreation-Union Facility at Epsilon College

Epsilon College is a private institution of 2800 students located in a
town of 13,000 people in the Midwest. Virtually all of the students
are full time, and most of them live on the campus in residence halls
and Greek houses. The college is reasonably selective.

Over a five-year period, Epsilon College's enrollment decreased
by two hundred students. Prospective students were concerned
about the high costs of attendance, especially when compared
with those of public institutions in the state. Moreover, the
admissions staff reported that some prospective students thought
there was not much to do at the college in this small town. The dean
of students at Epsilon had been in his job for three years and was
highly visible on the campus, frequently visiting with students in the
Commons, in residence halls, in Greek houses, and at a variety of
campus events. He loved working at Epsilon and was convinced
that students benefited greatly from the rich academic and student
life of the college. But he was concerned that the college union was
old and no longer an inviting meeting place for students and faculty

on the campus. Most student social life took place in the Greek houses. He was also concerned that the only place for indoor student exercise was the old college gym, which was also used by the various college intercollegiate sports teams, and was not regularly available to students. The dean of students was convinced that the college needed a better facility to bring students and faculty together, but was aware that the administration at the college had been in place for a long time and did not see any real need for change. Nevertheless, he decided to take on this challenge.

Epsilon's president, a respected chemist and the person to whom the dean reported, had been in his position for twenty-two years. He did not have much personal contact with students. He occasionally expressed his concern to the dean about excessive drinking in the fraternity houses, but for the most part, he stayed out of student life issues. He was very active in fundraising for the college. The dean was determined to convince the president that the college was far behind the times in its non-academic student facilities. After a number of tries, he finally succeeded in getting the president to join him and the student government president on a day-long automobile trip to two similar colleges, both of which had recently completed new campus recreation centers. Both the president and the student government officer were impressed, not only with the facilities, but also with their popularity and heavy use by students, faculty, and staff. The dean was pleased that perhaps he may have opened some eyes.

He then sought the president's support for his effort to invite a diverse group of students, faculty, staff, and alumni to join a special committee to explore, study, and recommend improvements in campus facilities that could encourage personal interaction. The president made no promises for financial support, but he was impressed by the dean's enthusiasm and persistence, and eventually agreed to let the dean give it a try. The dean had no trouble in forming the special committee, which included two student government officers, a member of the faculty senate, the athletic director, the college union director, the college's associate business vice president, the student activities director, and a member of the development staff. The dean chose not to chair the group, but was very active with it, charging it to seek ways that the college could bring students and faculty together in informal ways and also to suggest ways to fund a needed facility if that is what is needed. He urged the committee to be innovative in its thinking, to invite experienced campus architects and consultants to advise it, and to visit other, similar campuses for models to consider. He assured the committee that he would work closely with it over the six months he gave them to complete their work, and reminded them that there was no guarantee that Epsilon College might approve any recommendations they chose to make. The committee was very enthusiastic about this opportunity to suggest changes at Epsilon. Very soon after the committee began its deliberations, their discussions became known across campus, and their open, weekly meetings were well attended by other members of the Epsilon community.

After several months of lively discussion and debate, the committee eagerly recommended to the dean that the current old student union be demolished and in its place, an innovative new campus center, consisting of extensive recreation functions, traditional student union space, and informal dining spaces, be constructed. The new center would be open eighteen hours per day and would be freely available to students, faculty, and staff. The purpose of the new center would be to serve as a friendly, healthy, accessible place for the Epsilon campus community to come together. They also recommended to the dean that the development office should immediately begin a five-year fundraising program for the new center, while also seeking out a major donor whose name might adorn the facility. To the dean's surprise, the student government officers volunteered to conduct a collegewide referendum designed to approve a modest new Campus Center fee. The dean and the student government officers knew that if the students themselves pledged their own money to support part of the costs of the center, this certainly would serve as a stimulus to alumni and friends of the college to become donors.

Discussion. The dean of students recognized a problem, worked hard to secure the support of his president, provided an enticing and beneficial vision of what could be done, and formed an influential, campuswide committee to consider the possibilities. He had earned his credibility in his first three years as a campus leader by his outgoing concern for students and his hard work on their behalf. He knew this process would take a long time and would face many obstacles over a period of years. Yet his strategy of persistence, involving many others, proceeding step by step and achieving small wins along the way, eventually resulted in a positive new facility for the campus.

A New Student Affairs Development Office

Zeta University is a prestigious public research institution of 26,000 students in the Northwest. It has an extensive student affairs organization, which includes most of the traditional departments, from admissions and housing to counseling, student life, and financial aid. It has a large graduate program as well and professional schools of law, medicine, nursing, and dentistry.

Financial support from the state legislature had decreased, resulting in tuition increases for students. There had been cutbacks in various academic programs, and in many cases, when faculty and staff had retired, their positions were not filled. There was a large and successful development program at Zeta, headed by a vice president, and despite the poor economy, the institution was considering a new, $1 billion, five-year fundraising campaign.

The student affairs vice president was new to Zeta, having been in her position for six months. She came to Zeta from the Midwest and had worked in administrative positions at other institutions for over twenty years. All of the current functions in student affairs at Zeta were funded from the regular institutional budget or from student fees. The vice president already had to deal with budget cuts in her first six months and was disappointed that the student affairs division had never had a role in the institution's fundraising program. While she knew that beginning a development office in her own division would be difficult, she saw this as something that needed to be pursued, and she began thinking about how to go about it.

After reading extensively, conferring with student affairs colleagues at other universities who already had development offices in their divisions, and discussing this with her senior staff, she decided to explore this idea with the vice president for development at Zeta. He was surprised but delighted to learn of her interest, because in his twelve years as vice president, no one from student affairs had ever approached him. He reminded the student affairs vice president about what she already knew—she would need the president's support, and there would surely be opposition expressed by the twelve college deans, who were very protective of their own development programs. She also knew that she would need professional staff for a student affairs development office and that it was very unlikely that any institutional support for such positions would be forthcoming. But, she was a persistent, determined leader, and she had many projects, programs, and facilities in mind that, if funded someday, could substantially improve the quality of student life and education at Zeta. She was strongly committed to this exciting possibility, despite the many obstacles.

After convincing her president that he should not stand in her way in this effort (with a wry smile, he wished her luck!) her next step was to discuss the idea in more detail with her own staff. She was right in expecting some reluctance from them, as this represented a significant change in how they viewed their traditional roles. She then invited two experienced consultants in student affairs fundraising to spend three days on campus with her and her staff, and she followed up their visits with several more discussions with her staff, as she knew it would take time for most of them to embrace this new direction and deal with the obvious risks of failure that it involved. Her next step was to solicit names of outstanding former student leaders at Zeta who remained well known to many of her student affairs staff. She then invited 15 of them to a special weekend meeting on campus. Her purpose was to ask for their advice on ways to improve the quality of student life at Zeta. To her considerable pleasure, the Zeta graduates who were invited to this meeting responded with enthusiasm. Many asked, "Why has it taken you so long to ask us?" They felt that their involvement in leadership and student life when they were in school was, and still remained, a significant part of their education, and they expressed their eagerness to help. The vice president was greatly encouraged by this response, and with her staff began to expand their thinking about graduates and friends of the university who might have similar interests and feelings about student life issues.

She shared what she had done with the vice president for development, who was impressed with her work to date. He encouraged her to continue with it and offered the support of his staff. She knew she would have to begin slowly, and achieving any success would require patience and small steps. Now, she knew she had to find a way to fund a full-time development position in her office. She was able to do this by transferring funding for two half-time positions in the two major auxiliaries in her division (housing and the health service) to her office, and with the advice and assistance of the vice president for development, she hired a full-time student affairs development officer. Concurrently with this, she invited a group of alumni and friends of the institution to serve on the first Student Affairs Development Council. In the next several months, she, the council, and her staff outlined their strategies for moving forward. She knew this was a long-term, risky venture, with no guarantee for success, and also realized that this represented a significant change within student affairs at Zeta, as well as a test of her own leadership.

Discussion. The vice president of student affairs knew that this change was something she could not do alone. Thus, her strategy from the beginning was to know the issues and obstacles, learn everything she could about fundraising, help her own staff gain an understanding of the issue and what its potential might be for the division, and, especially, to involve significant others in the process. This venture would take many years to demonstrate its success, but she had the persistence and determination to pursue it, and she felt that she had helped lay the groundwork to make it happen.

Conclusion

Student affairs administrators are responsible for initiating change that can improve student learning, enhance the quality of facilities, services, and programs, and enrich the quality of student life on their campuses. It is a difficult, challenging, messy, competitive, and often lengthy process that requires student affairs administrators to demonstrate their knowledge, skills, determination, courage, and patience. In this process, they face significant challenges, such as decreasing institutional funds, increased demands for services, increased public scrutiny, changing patterns of institutional governance, myths about how change actually occurs, changing students, and increasing demands for online services. While these challenges may seem daunting, student affairs administrators have many resources available to them, including facilities, their own staff and students, faculty, money, and their community. They also can benefit from the insights gained from their knowledge of organizational theories, such as those described by O'Toole, Kotter, Schein, Kouzes and Posner, and others. They can also learn about how to use resources effectively to effect change by studying how student affairs leaders at other campuses succeeded in similar efforts.

Securing and using resources is key to the success of student affairs administrators. If adequate resources cannot be obtained, or if available resources are not used wisely, educational opportunities for students will be diminished. Student affairs administrators do not just "manage" resources—they also need to understand that their role is to make change happen by obtaining more resources and using them effectively. In this process, they must be realistic about the problems and obstacles they face, learn from the valuable insights provided by research about organizational change, know and be passionate about what they can do to improve student learning opportunities, and be determined and persistent in their role as leaders.

Reflection Questions

1. As a student affairs administrator interested in change, how do I develop the skills necessary to become an effective leader?

2. How are staff, faculty, students, provosts, and presidents best approached regarding change?

3. Who decides what changes are needed?

4. Am I willing to take the risks necessary for real change to occur?

5. What are the consequences if a significant change I have worked to bring about fails or is rejected?

6. Should I adjust my strategy, depending on the history and nature of the groups with whom I am working?

4

Utilizing Technology
in Search of Success

Processes, including change, are often described as either evolutionary or revolutionary. Evolutionary change is marked by gradual realignment; revolutionary change is rapid and transformative (Burke, 2007). The former can allow for more contemplative development of change with less stress, but the pace may be inadequate to meet the needs at hand. The latter can reframe and revitalize a community or organization; it can also disrupt a community or organization. Just as many in student affairs perceive the development of the trinity of intellectual resources of our profession (foundational documents, theories, and literature) as evolutionary, a goodly number would describe technological innovation as a revolutionary process.

This chapter will address technology as a resource through which student affairs professionals can shape both evolutionary and revolutionary change in programs and services in support of the success of the students and institutions they serve, as well as in their own professional development and support for the student affairs profession as a whole. The terms *technology, computer-mediated communication,* and *social media* are used frequently (and at some points interchangeably) in this chapter, so it may be helpful at the outset to offer brief working definitions for all three. *Technology* is a broad term and is used in this chapter to refer to both software and hardware as well as the myriad ways in which they are used to support educational and administrative activities in higher education. Mobile applications for use on pads, tablets, and smartphones are a form of technology at the forefront of a great deal of activity with significant potential to contribute to change in a number of arenas of campus life. *Computer-mediated communication* also includes both software and hardware dimensions but refers to a specific realm of the use of technology—the sharing of information or perspective using technology. Some of us remember old school e-communication such as electronic bulletin boards and chat rooms. Email and its e-cousin texting are contemporary ubiquitous forms. *Social media* is a form of computer-mediated communication that has a network or social group element. Virtual networks such as Twitter, Instagram, and Facebook are contemporary examples.

The chapter opens with a discussion of the technological context within which student affairs professionals serve. Next, a number of strategies and questions are shared for consideration in making use of technology to shape desired change. The chapter also includes several case studies offering an opportunity for readers to consider the application of information from the chapter to professional practice, and the chapter closes with reflective questions that provide an opportunity for readers to give thought to their own experiences and insights related to change and technology.

Everything All the Time

The Eagles' hit single "Life in the Fast Lane" includes the lyric, "Life in the fast lane. Everything all the time" (Walsh, Frey, and Henley, 1976). That seems apt when giving thought to the place of technology in modern life. Computing and computer-mediated communication (the use of computers and computer networks to send and receive messages, videos, and other types of communication) have become seemingly ubiquitous, and the rapidity with which new technologies emerge and recede is dizzying. Gupta (2011) gives voice to this perspective when observing, "Many other industrial events and advancements in the history of mankind took place at a steady and understandable pace. Technology, however, was behind the scenes one day and in our faces the next."

However, in his fascinating look at the history of the intersection between technology and student affairs, Guidry makes the case that consideration of technological innovation is not completely new in student affairs. He notes that there was mention of "mechanical devices" as early as 1928 in the profession's literature (Guidry, 2012b) and discussion of technological skills as a competency in student affairs in the 1970s (Guidry, 2012a).

While at least present, such references were not commonplace until the use of computers became commonplace in work settings and then rapidly accelerated as computers became common in households—and residence halls—as the twentieth century came to a close.

There can be little doubt that the continuing expansion of computer-mediated communication is driving a great deal of activity in higher education, including student affairs (Logan, Gross, Junco, and Oliver, 2011). Student affairs professionals and others in higher education experience this in their observations of and interaction with students, in their administrative or teaching practices, and in their professional development activities.

Students

Students enrolled in colleges and universities today are arguably one of the groups most engaged in computing and computer-mediated communication (Duderstadt, 2002; Oblinger and Oblinger, 2005). Kruger (2009, p. 587) observes, "The extent to which computers, the Internet, and all forms of technology are woven into the fabric of college student lives has been well documented by the popular media and in such national research projects as the Pew Internet and American Life Project." However, it is important to note that, while observations regarding wide and pervasive adoption of technology may be true of students on the whole, some significant differences exist in this regard within the broad spectrum of people enrolled as students (Drake, 2013; Aviles, Phillips, Rosenblatt, and Vargas, 2005) when it comes to access, ease, and interest regarding technology.

Kruger's (2005) comment regarding the fabric of student lives is interesting inasmuch as it implies that students' use of technology is incorporated into their brick-and-mortar or real-world lives. That assertion is supported by the findings by Martínez Alemán and Wartman (2011) in their study of student use of social media. They found,

> College and university students inhabit and populate hybrid worlds. Whether commuting to campus or living on campus in residence halls, students readily navigate and travel both real-world and online environments. Living in a century in which technological advances enable easy, quick, and highly developed computer-mediated communication, our students effortlessly execute the many functions of their academic and social lives in and through online spaces that are informed by and affect their real-world experiences. (p. 515)

A group of senior student affairs officers conducting an exploratory qualitative study of the ways in which students define, seek, and value community (Grieve, Hopkins, McClellan, Sachs, and Wong, 2011) yielded similar results with regard to students views on community in cyberspace. The hundreds of students across the country who participated in focus group interviews as part of the study were fairly clear. They tend to use computer-mediated communication more to extend existing real-world communities as opposed to using it to create or join new communities in cyberspace.

While the use of technology offers students a great number of beneficial opportunities, there are also potential problems related to such use. Cole-Avent (2008, p. 1) states, "the profession has also witnessed the negative aspects of information technology including legal, ethical and institutional policy issues that address privacy, intellectual property and copyright infringement, and Internet addiction (Kruger, 2005)." Recent reports have also provided indication of potential problems for students with time management (Gemmill and Peterson, 2006), online bullying (Laster, 2010), online gambling (Petry and Weinstock, 2007), and more associated with their engagement with technology.

Administrative and Teaching Practices

Kruger asserts, "Information technology has altered virtually every business practice within higher education during the past decade. While higher education has never achieved the paperless office that was promised in the early years of this latest technology revolution, technology advances have transformed the majority of administrative functions" (2009, p. 592). A simple review of daily life on campus will reveal that technology is shaping both administrative and teaching practices.

Exploring which colleges to attend, applying to college, applying for financial aid, registering for classes, checking or paying a university account, checking grades, receiving announcements about events or situations on campus, getting academic assistance, making an appointment with an advisor or professor, taking a course or submitting work for a course; conducting research, tracking degree progress, applying to graduate, and communicating with staff and faculty are just some of the ways in which today's students interact with their university using technology.

In addition to student expectations, the following are just a few of the ways staff and faculty use technology in the course of functions related to their roles: explore colleges at which to work, apply for positions, sign up for or check on benefits, submit vacation requests, share work product, receive announcements about events or situations on campus, reserve rooms for programs or classes, offer programs or courses, assess programs or courses, and communicate with students.

Specifically with regard to student affairs, Cole-Avent (2008, p. 1) observes,

> Information technology has positively contributed to college student affairs work through environments that support community development via social and professional networking (Moneta, 2005), web-based student services (Shea, 2005), and assessment and evaluation (Hanson, 1997), resulting in the potential increased efficiency of administrative processes and services.

Developments in technology have also shaped teaching and learning. Duderstadt (2002) argues that students' experience with technology has shaped them as learners and requires appropriate responses in teaching methods. Kruger (2005) and colleagues describe a number of strategies for using a variety of technologies to enhance student learning. Tarantino, McDonough, and Hua (2013) provide a very helpful overview of some of the ways in which student engagement in social media can be integrated into their learning experience.

> Social media, Internet-based tools that promote collaboration and information sharing (Junco, Helbergert, and Loken, 2011), can be used in academic settings to promote student engagement and facilitate better student learning (Kabilan, Ahmad, and Abidin, 2010). Because student engagement represents the time and effort that students invest in collaborative and educational activities (Kuh, 2001), it is often linked with the achievement of positive student learning outcomes, such as critical thinking and individual student development (Carini, Kuh, and Klein, 2006; Kuh, 1993).

At least one study indicates there is some evidence that faculty members are making increasing use of technology in their research activities (Straumsheim, 2013). Ithaka S+R's report notes that 40 percent of responding faculty stated they use general search engines when initiating their exploration of a topic, though three-quarters of respondents identified libraries as a central resource. This stands in interesting contrast to findings by Smith, Salaway, and Caruso (2009) reflecting that nearly 80 percent of students indicate their first choice of research resource is the Internet. There is less evidence that faculty members are being as quick to adapt technology into their teaching tools (Straumsheim, 2013).

Professional Development Activities

Professional development activities comprise another area of the student affairs profession that is being increasingly influenced by the adoption of new technology. In addition to self-directed or institutionally sponsored activities, professional associations, trade groups associated with the profession, and professional media are all important sources of professional development. Traditional programming formats utilized by these groups include newsletters and workshops, conferences, and journals and other publications. Each of these is being reshaped by technology.

Student affairs associations have for years offered program sessions, workshops, and published materials designed to help student affairs professionals develop their technological skills and consider the adoption of technology in their professional practice. It has been noted, however, that there is much more that can and should be done with regard to incorporating computer-mediated communication into professional development in student affairs (Leduc, 2011; Stoller, 2008).

It is interesting to note that at the time this book is being written the professional associations that have a membership with substantial proportions of graduate students and new professionals appear to have integrated their discussions of technology into the fabric of their programs and services. This may reflect generational differences in ability, familiarity, and perceived value when it comes to utilizing technology.

Conferences and drive-in workshops are principal components of the professional development services offered by associations for their members, and both reflect changes in technology. The program sessions make use of advanced software for presenting (using Prezi, for example), including people who are at other locations (using Skype, for example), and sharing content with people in other sessions at the conference and those outside the conference (using Twitter, for example).

It is not just that traditional conference and workshop experiences are being shaped by the expanding use of technology; technology is giving rise to new types of professional gatherings. One example is informal networking and professional development through informal conversations via social media. Twitter is one venue for such conversations, which are marked and organized by hashtags such as #sachat or #MSAchat. Tweet ups are gatherings of individuals who are connected in one or another via Twitter. New student affairs professionals in the Los Angeles area might connect via Twitter as a result of participating in one or more of the ongoing student affairs conversations and then organize a Tweet up in a park, pub, or place of mutual interest.

While it is difficult (and arguably antithetical to the culture of cybercitizens) to credit a single individual with a particular innovation in social media, Ed Cabellon probably deserves at least the lion's share of recognition for bringing forth the unconference (Cabellon, 2013a). An unconference is similar to a Tweet up in that it is driven by like-minded individuals (those in student affairs interested in technology, in the case of Cabellon's unconferences) who have come together over social media, but they are different in that once in the location the participants take part in something akin to a traditional drive-in workshop—sans the professional association or other institutional organizing agent.

The impact of technology on student affairs professional development activities goes beyond merely conferences and meetings. There are professional ejournals and eresources generated by formally structured organizations. Examples include *The Journal of Technology in Student Affairs* (StudentAffairs.com, 2013), *Student Affairs and Technology Blog* (Inside Higher Ed, 2013), or the National Association of Student Personnel Administrators (NASPA) Technology Knowledge Community website (NASPA, 2013). Thanks to the relatively inexpensive costs of hosting websites and free access to networking via social media, there are also technology-based professional development resources that emerge organically from like-minded groups of individuals. The Student Affairs Women Talk Tech (2013) website and blog came about in this fashion. As noted on their About page, "We [the women who created Student Affairs Women Talk Tech] are a group of female student affairs professionals working in a variety of fields with a passion for technology. This blog is designed as a forum for women in student affairs with an interest in technology. We focus on showcasing the women who are doing things with technology in the field of student affairs, and talking about some of the unique issues that face women as we break into a formerly male-dominated area."

Whether by intention or as the result of oversight, the cyberspace artifacts one produces (messages, photos, or publications for example) or the artifacts that others produce that somehow reference you (all those already mentioned, as well as reviews, for example) produce what can be thought of as a digital footprint. That footprint can impact positively or negatively on a student affairs professional's career (Cabellon, 2013b; Olsen, 2013).

Personal branding. Whereas professional development is about developing one's knowledge and skills through pursuing learning opportunities, personal branding is about packaging one's knowledge, skills, and professional experiences for the purposes of promoting one's professional reputation and career. The notion of personal branding as a form of professional development has received a great deal of attention in the popular media (see for example Doyle, 2013; Kang, 2013; Linkedin.com, 2013; Quast, 2012). There is even a Personal Branding for Dummies (Chritton, 2012). While some may find the notion of those working in higher education marketing themselves to be off-putting (Hacker, 2011), it is not surprising that student affairs professionals, too, are taking an interest in personal branding or that they are using technology as a tool to advance their personal branding (Larsen and Pasquini, 2011; Leduc, 2011; Stoller, 2012). Leduc (2011) makes the important observation that student affairs professionals ought to be mindful of their own personal brand, and they should not lose sight of the role they can play in helping students learn about personal branding.

The State of Student Affairs and Technological Innovation

As evidenced in the previous section, there can be little doubt that technology is driving change across a broad variety of dimensions of the human experience. This includes higher education, where technological innovation is both being driven and is driving. Within higher education, there is evidence that the work and careers of student affairs professionals are being shaped in substantial ways by their engagement with computer-mediated communication. However, despite signs of some interesting activity, the results of student affairs' engagement with technology can best be described as mixed. Cole-Avent (2008, p. 1) offers a succinct summary of the situation.

> The college student affairs profession has constantly adapted to the ever-changing environment within higher education. The profession has remained current ahead of the trends in crisis management, student learning, collaboration with academic affairs, and professional standards. Traditionally known within higher education

for their expertise in those areas, along with student development and innovative programming, college student affairs professionals cannot claim the same expertise in the area of information technology.

While there are a growing number of newer student affairs professionals (and some in mid- and senior-level positions) who are actively making use of computer-mediated communication, many in the profession feel overwhelmed by technology (Graham, 2011; Gupta, 2001; Moneta, 2005). Student Affairs at Weber State offers an example of how a group of student affairs colleagues are taking this issue head-on. Their Tech Trivia staff development program (Weber State University, 2013) includes an online resource, education outreach, and a bit of play to relieve stress.

A Simple Question

Eric Stoller, a critical and thoughtful advocate for the ways in which student affairs professionals should (and should not) make use of technology in changing programs and services, offers a succinct and straightforward tip. He suggests, "The secret to being an avid student affairs techie is very simple. Whenever/wherever you notice a new technology solution, thought piece, or tech-based recommendation, always ask a question: Is this relevant to the work that I do in student affairs?"

Drawing on earlier work by Upcraft and Terenzini (1999), Upcraft and Goldsmith (2000) provide a more expansive set of questions for considering the implications of integrating technology into professional practice. It includes

1. How will the philosophy and goals of student affairs be affected?

2. How can student affairs use the positive aspects of technology while minimizing the negative aspects?

3. How can we ensure that technology will not depersonalize the campus and reduce student and faculty contact?

4. How does technology affect our mission? What responsibility, if any, do we have to deliver student services and programs to students learning at a distance? How will these services and programs differ from those offered in a traditional campus setting?

5. How can we ensure that students with less accessibility to computer resources will not be disadvantaged?

6. How does student affairs keep up with technological advances and how will they be funded? (pp. 223–227)

Beware the Junkyard of Next Big Things

While considering the implications and possibilities that technology may have for bringing about a desired change is important, predicting the future as it relates to technology can be difficult if not impossible. The goal and the focus should be framed in terms of the desired outcome and not the specific intended vehicle of delivery.

The landscape of higher education is littered with the detritus of the "next big things." Those who have served in higher education for several years are likely to recall the time when colleges sought to provide every student with a particular type of computer, and it is likely that those same colleagues will be aware of how quickly colleges moved away from that approach because students preferred to make their own choice related to such an important purchase. More recently, the case of Massive Open Online Courses (or MOOCs) in higher education can serve as a helpful example of the potential and perils of technological innovation as it relates to teaching and learning. After entering into the broad discourse of higher education in Fall 2011, MOOCs quickly became heralded as the next big thing in higher education with a string of particularly favorable articles, columns, and presentations (Association of

Governing Boards of Universities and Colleges, 2013). No less an authority than William Bowen, president emeritus of the Andrew W. Mellon Foundation and former president of Princeton University, expressed the belief that MOOCs hold remarkable promise (Bowen, 2013). However, almost at the same time, data began to emerge indicating that perhaps they were not all that their proponents had hoped. Questions surfaced about how attractive MOOCs are to students (Kolowich, 2013a), how students fare in them (Hiltzik, 2013), and whether or not faculty are inclined to embed their intellectual property in them (Guthrie, 2013). While it may be too early to declare them dead, it is clear that the notion of MOOCs as the technological cure-all for higher education has been severely damaged (Kolowich, 2013b).

While it may not be necessary to make use of all the latest bells and whistles to convey content, it is essential to assure that content is current. Inaccurate or incomplete information, broken hyperlinks (or links to sites no longer in existence), or yesterday's news are all indicators to users—students or otherwise—that little if any attention or value is being placed on communicating with them.

Case Studies

What might using technology to address challenges and opportunities in student affairs look like? The following case studies are intended to help address that question.

Badlands University

Badlands University, part of the state's higher education system, is a small baccalaureate institution situated in a rugged rural area. Many of the institution's students are first generation learners who come from farming and ranching families spread across the region, and few of them have ever traveled outside of the area.

The university had recently welcomed a new chancellor. One of her goals was encouraging students to travel beyond the region for learning opportunities. She looked to the vice chancellor for academic affairs and the vice chancellor for student life for leadership in achieving those goals, as they had a history of collaborating on initiatives at Badlands University.

As a first step, the two vice chancellors approached the Student Government Association very early in the new school year to invite them to participate in a project designed to understand where in the world students might want to go. At the suggestion of the student leaders, all members of the student body were encouraged to create short videos (thirty seconds or less) in which they described where they would like to visit if they had the chance to travel as part of an academic experience and what they would hope to learn. Students were told the videos would be posted to a Facebook page that would be open for everyone to see as well as shared via Twitter using a special hashtag. They were also informed that the chancellor of Badlands had agreed to find funding to support some of the proposed trips. Videos, made with a variety of devices, were submitted by email. Once posted, they were reviewed by a team of students, student affairs professionals, and faculty members who scanned for destinations or learning goals that were shared by a number of students. The team identified a number of such destinations and themes, drew up a set of notes about them, and selected several videos associated with each one.

The team presented their findings to the chancellor, vice chancellors, and student and faculty leaders at the end of the first term. The group identified several destinations or themes that they thought represented great learning opportunities in which students would be interested and for which faculty sponsors could be identified. Faculty members were approached about offering one-credit spring break course trips over spring break to various destinations. The chancellor agreed to waive tuition for these courses, to make funding available to compensate faculty, and to help identify other funding (either gift aid or other aid) for students who need help with resources for the trips.

Badlands University created travel blogs for each of the trips, and student learning on the trips was evaluated (and graded) based on participation in those blogs. Students were encouraged to post both text and digital images. Those who had access to Twitter or Facebook could earn extra credit by posting tweets throughout their trip. Students who did not go on the trips were encouraged to respond to the social media posts, and those who did received a T-shirt and note of thanks from the chancellor acknowledging their participation in the project.

One of the trips was made to a major city where students were encouraged to explore cultural diversity. Students traveled by bus and stayed in a youth hostel. Another group engaged in a service trip to a national park, where they helped with a variety of projects and were invited to reflect on how to attract more interest in and support for public parks. The third group traveled by rail to a mid-sized city where they visited arts agencies and local artists. Their charge was investigating the role of artistic expression in the life of a community.

Once back on campus, the faculty hosted and student participants presented a program for the community, both campus and local, regarding their experiences. Their enthusiasm for the experience, coupled with the evidence of their learning, provided ample evidence of the value of the program. The program is well positioned to continue in the coming years.

Discussion. While it is true that bringing about the change described in this case study did require a modest investment of money and employee time, it also tapped into the incredibly powerful (and free) resource that students represent. The two vice chancellors' decision to involve student leadership in the early stages of planning led them quickly to the potential uses of technology and social media in bringing about the change in which the chancellor was interested. Engaging students, both undergraduate and graduate, regarding uses of technology, computer-mediated communication, and social media to improve services and programs can help tap into their tremendous energy, information, and insights while also providing invaluable learning experiences.

The program used technology in several ways to help achieve progress toward the strategic objective of encouraging students to consider the world beyond their immediate community. The video contest tapped into students' creativity and interest in technology. The use of blogs and Twitter provided opportunities for students to reflect on their experiences and to share them with students who could not or had not chosen to take part in the actual trips. For some students, the opportunity to engage the broader world through technology from the relative safety of their home provided them with a first step toward actually taking part in a future trip.

It is important to note the careful consideration given by the two vice chancellors to help assure opportunities for folks with differing resources of funding and time to participate. Technology has become commonplace, and it is often assumed (and even expected) that people will have access to a smartphone and big data plans. Such assumptions need to be challenged as part of the planning process for change.

Social University

The senior student affairs officer (SSAO) at Social State University (a midwestern mid-sized private institution whose students are mostly commuters) was proud of the accomplishments of the division. Their programs and services were held in high regard by students, staff, and faculty, and student affairs was respected as an active partner in many of the university's major initiatives.

That said, student participation in the programs and services could have been higher. Surveys of the students indicated one reason people did not participate is that they were unaware of the opportunities, and another reason is that the programs were offered on days or at times when they were not available. The SSAO believed that social media might be a helpful way of addressing both of these concerns, despite having limited personal involvement in social media himself.

Engagement with technology was uneven across the units in the division. Some were highly engaged, making use of computer-mediated communication in a variety of interesting and effective ways. Other units were making modest or moderate use of technology, focusing on email or fairly traditional websites. Still other units, though few in number, were making little if any use of social media or other technology.

The SSAO invited three staff members in the division, each from a different department and each already fairly active in social media, to participate in a webinar being offered on using social media in student affairs. The team was also charged with surveying the division regarding their current use of computer-mediated communication. The trio was asked to prepare recommendations for the division based on their own experiences, information from the webinar, and results from the survey. After having been shared with the SSAO, the results were presented by the three staff members at a divisionwide meeting. The SSAO also invited the institution's web and social media point person, key student para-professionals who were active online, and some student leaders to the presentation. A robust conversation took place in which both strategic, practical, and philosophical issues related to the use of social media were addressed. Based on this conversation, the SSAO worked with division heads in the unit to outline some general expectations for the division with regard to the use of social media to increased outreach to students and to make it possible for students with scheduling conflicts to review content from programs they have to miss.

Units created office Facebook pages and Twitter accounts. Some also created Pinterest boards or added blogs to their office pages. As part of exploring how to make greater use of social media, a few departments (such as Student Records and Academic Testing) came to the realization that the use of social media would not really contribute to greater participation or quality in their programs and services. However, these units identified opportunities to utilize web-based videos as a means to offer helpful information to their constituents regardless of their availability to make it to a formal program, and these units began planning to develop, implement, and deploy such videos.

The group that planned the big kickoff event for entering students decided to create display boards with the Quick Response (QR) codes for the website and Facebook page for each of the units participating in the Activities Fair. They also created boards with QR codes to web pages that had been created listing resources or schedules related to various topics (for example, tutoring and study skills, health and recreation, etc.), and those boards were placed throughout the various activities of the day. Finally, they encouraged students to come to the kickoff day prepared to use Twitter to share their experiences using the hashtag #SocialNow. All those who contributed to the hashtag conversation received a T-shirt emblazoned with the #SocialNow phrase, and students were encouraged to use that hashtag throughout the year to tweet about their experiences at Social University programs or events.

The social media initiative is very new at Social University so robust data are not yet available regarding the impact of the program. However, there is some early evidence that the program is making a positive difference in several ways. Student organizations and student affairs offices are cross-posting, sharing, and retweeting announcements helping to assure that word of programs and services is being shared widely. Student organizations and staff programmers are commenting that they are seeing new faces at their programs and that participation is up at a number of programs. Staff members in student affairs are also commenting on the increased number of questions and comments they are receiving now that their department is engaging students via social media. There is some concern about adjusting the volume of these interactions, but the general consensus is that the additional contact offers potential for helping address student inquiries or concerns more quickly. One other concern is that traffic using the #SocialNow hashtag has slowed, and the staff is talking with students about what meaning to make of that.

Discussion. The case of Social University offers the important lesson that using technology, computer-mediated communication, and social media to bring about change is most likely to succeed when undertaken collectively rather than in isolation. When it comes to identifying leadership for a student affairs division's technology-related growth, it is difficult to imagine one person keeping up with the astounding pace of change and innovation. A team-based leadership approach offers greater promise. Given that engagement with technology may correlate with generation (Stone, 2010), such a team-based approach could have the added benefit of providing a way of offering new professionals with an important shared assignment with a divisional scope of responsibility—a great opportunity for them to further their own professional development.

Similarly, any one unit in student affairs at Social University might have decided to become more active and purposeful with regard to their use of social media, but the decision of the division to engage in this activity as a whole improves the likelihood that the goal of increased participation in programs and services will be met.

Finally, and in an interesting counterpoint to the notion of collective action, Social University's experience illustrates that individual units can and should have the opportunity to adapt goals and plans to best suit their individual circumstances. Those units that came to realize that utilization of social media would not improve rates of participation in their programs and services did not simply decide to opt out of the division's communication program; they took the initiative to identify ways in which other forms of technology might help them achieve important goals with regard to improving service.

Professional Presence

The three staff members of Social University who played a leadership role in helping change the culture of student affairs regarding
social media had an impact in ways that even they did not see
coming. The SSAO, who previously had only moderate engagement with technology, realized that it was important to model the
behavior that was being encouraged across the units. She decided to
develop her professional presence online.

Using information shared by the staff members and gleaned
through a review of various blogs and websites related to student
affairs and technology, the SSAO gathered enough information to
develop a plan. That plan reflected recognition on the part of the
SSAO that they were unlikely to be active daily on social media but
would occasionally update content or provide new content. Hence,
the plan included Twitter and Pinterest accounts and a website with
a blog. The website featured information about the SSAO, links to
their social media presence, and links to their publications. In
addition, the SSAO included a couple of pages focused on things
she enjoys or finds interesting and that may be of interest to others.

Almost immediately the SSAO began to have followers on both
the Twitter and Pinterest accounts. The first blog posted drew a
number of positive comments. The SSAO realized it might be
helpful to others to offer links to interesting student affairs blogs or
pages, and a number of them linked back in return. As the network
of connections grew, the SSAO realized how much more information about student affairs and higher education was available to her
on a daily basis. Some of this information was shared within the
Social University student affairs division to help encourage thinking
about issues, opportunities, programs, and services. Some of the
information was passed on through social media to wider networks.
While the SSAO had to make some adjustments in time management to make room for this new activity, the return on the
investment of time seemed well worth it.

Discussion. This case helps us keep in mind that sometimes the change we seek is in ourselves. The SSAO's choice to heed the advice of her staff with regard to personal involvement and investment in the use of technology yielded very positive outcomes. We say it all the time to our students, but it is advice we would do well to keep in mind in our own practice. There is no substitute for getting involved. It is arguably the case that there are generational differences when it comes to both knowledge and comfort related to interacting with and through technology. That said, given the degree to which students (and staff and faculty) are engaged with technology, it is well past time to abandon being a Luddite when it comes to computing, computer-mediated communication, and social media.

Conclusion

Leduc (2011) notes, "As the topic of social media becomes more common area of focus within our offices and our field, we must ask ourselves who will drive the conversations around the use, research, best practices, integration, and concerns surrounding it." The same can be said of the broader realm of technology, and one can look to Gupta's earlier comments about technology for an answer. He observes, "Some of us will be quarterbacks in the technology field but all of us must be players. The choice has already been made for us!" In other words, no matter what our position or role in the student affairs profession, there are potential benefits to our utilizing technology as a resource in our work and in our career. Framing his observations in the context of the core elements of professional practice in student affairs, Cabellon (2013) sagely offers, "Remember, because we have the privilege of working in Higher Education, we also have a greater responsibility to use online communication tools to share the best of what is happening on our campuses; ask each other for help around common challenges; and create connections for our students and fellow staff to facilitate learning and growth. We all have stories to share . . . let's spend more time on sharing them."

It is worthwhile to remember that addressing the challenge or opportunity ahead is the goal of whatever effort will be put forth. Technology, no matter how fascinating, new, or popular it may be, is in the end simply one of many devices that might contribute to achieving that goal. It does not help to pick the wrong tool for the right job. Technology is a wonderful resource for some challenges and opportunities; it is not a suitable tool for all them. When it comes time to congratulate or console, while it is possible to use technology to communicate a message, there is no substitute for a human handshake or hug.

Reflective Questions

1. What are your thoughts regarding appropriate uses of technology, computer-mediated communication, and social media in professional practice in student affairs?

2. How do you assess the level of engagement and effectiveness of your department, division, and institution in using technology, computer-mediated communication, and social media?

3. What are your supervisor's views on the use of technology, computer-mediated communication, and social media? How do you know those are their views? Have the two of you discussed it? Is there other evidence on which you can draw?

4. What are you doing to improve your knowledge and skill set related to technology?

5. What are your observations with regard to the ways in which technology, computer-mediated communication, and social media can be used to enhance student learning? Are there potential negative consequences for student learning in your view?

6. How much is known about how students at your institution are engaging with technology, computer-mediated communication, and social media? Who has particular expertise or interest that you might tap? What can they help you understand about students' expectations (or tolerances) related to the university being in their cyberworld?

7. Can you identify an instance when you attempted to make use of technology, computer-mediated communication, or social media to bring about a change on your campus? How was that effort received? What was the result of the effort? If you are unable to identify such an instance, why is that the case?

5

Advocating for Some Students While Serving All Students

William Monat, the former president of Northern Illinois University, once observed that an important role for student affairs professionals is to "speak up for student interests but never speak down to the student" (1985, p. 57). He did not suggest that student affairs professionals always agree with students or that they only deal with the issues that students bring forward. Rather he believed that student affairs had a special responsibility to speak up for student interests and concerns particularly in those venues where they are unable to speak for themselves. His powerful advice remains relevant to the work student affairs continues to do on countless campuses across this country and the world.

Being able to speak up for students has become, however, a much more difficult task than it was when his words were written. Students in higher education have become much more diverse on many dimensions: ethnicity, age, preparation for college, sexual identity and sexual orientation, race, gender, religious beliefs. physical abilities, interests, motivation to enroll in college, financial circumstances, and psychological issues are but a few examples of student diversity. Several factors have contributed to creating the diverse student bodies that populate the campuses of American higher education institutions. These include the economic needs of the country, federal programs to support the disadvantaged, the quest for equality in American society, the aging of America, and access to educational opportunities for the disabled. The challenge of advocating for some while serving all brings with it complex questions that at times seem difficult to fairly balance as concerns surface and priorities change.

For example, while many colleges and universities have special programs and support systems for students who are underprepared for college work, how many have intentional and focused programs for those who are prepared to tackle the academic challenges ahead? Do those students have other issues and concerns that should be addressed? At one private institution the governing board was interested in increasing the number of National Merit Scholars who enrolled at the institution. As one of the intentional outreach efforts to this group of students, the vice president for student affairs wrote individual letters to each National Merit Scholar who was admitted and personally invited him or her to participate in the freshman leadership program. For the next three years the capture rate for such scholars steadily increased. As a group, the scholars cited one of the top reasons for enrolling at the institution was that the institution identified them as potential leaders as well as scholars. This was a successful venture, but it took time and effort to make it happen. That time and effort could have been spent in support of other groups of students.

This chapter addresses the many movements, social causes, statutes, court decisions, and societal changes that helped bring diversity in its many forms to American higher education. Then the chapter addresses the strategies that have been employed to attempt to build a diverse and supportive community for all students. It then presents case studies dealing with the real challenges a more diverse community brings to any campus. The chapter closes with a series of reflective questions for readers to ponder as they work with an increasingly diverse student body.

There are so many easily identified needs in our diverse student bodies. Identifying unmet needs of students and then meeting them is difficult, particularly in times of restricted budgets and changing societal expectations for higher education. What responsibility do student affairs professionals have to speak up for *all* students while meeting the unique needs of specific subpopulations? The answer to that question may be different depending on the history and traditions of the institution and the composition of the student body. An initial step for any student affairs professional involves understanding how higher education, in general, and the specific institution where they are employed grew more diverse.

Understanding How American Higher Education Became Diverse

The question of serving some or serving all has been an issue in American higher education for some time. Several factors have contributed to creating the diverse student bodies that now populate the campuses of American higher education institutions. Looking beyond a simple analysis of one group versus another or one group versus the whole, McClellan and Larimore (2009) caution student affairs professionals to be sensitive to the diversity within population groupings and to take the time to understand those differences as well. With that caveat in mind, the following brief summaries provide a broad description of the causes of diversity on the contemporary college campus.

Economic Needs of the Country

A major force in changing the face of American higher education from that of education for the elite or religious reasons was the creation of the Land Grant institutions across America (Morrill Acts of 1862 and 1890). The Morrill Act "Provided support in every state for at least one college where the leading objective was to "teach such branches if learning as are related to agriculture and the mechanical arts" (Knock, 1985, p. 20). Those institutions changed not only who came to college but also the reasons why students were enrolled. The state university became an important part of American higher education and was supplemented by the growth of community colleges to meet the needs of business and industry and local communities (Knock, 1985). While private institutions continued to meet important needs in education, the rapid growth of public institutions both at the senior and community college level brought new and different students with different goals to higher education.

Federal Support for the Disadvantaged

Federal program support for disadvantaged students began in 1964 with the creation of the Upward Bound programs as part of President Johnson's War on Poverty. Through competitive applications a major focus was placed on preparing underprepared students for higher education. The program was expanded with Talent Search in 1965 and in 1968 by the creation for Student Support Services. These programs were focused on disadvantaged students and were authorized initiation through the Economic Opportunity Act of 1964 and later created as part of the Higher Education Act in 1981 (United States Department of Education, 2011). Over the years the initial TRIO programs were expanded to include Educational Opportunity Centers through the Higher Education Act of 1972. In 1976, the Education Amendments authorized the Training Program for Federal TRIO Programs and in 1986 the Ronald E. McNair Post-Baccalaureate Achievement Program. In 1990, the department created the Upward Bound Math/Science Education Program to address the need for improved math and science education. Finally, in the Omnibus Appropriation Act of 2001 amended the Student Support Services program to permit the use of program funds for direct financial assistance to current students enrolled in Student Support Services who were also receiving Federal Pell grants (United States Department of Education, September 2011).

Although these programs all had income criteria for participation and were not present on all college campuses, they were forerunners of other efforts to meet the needs of underrepresented students with the higher education system in the United States. These programs brought the first real wave of underrepresented students to institutions of higher education across the country, and the Pell Grant program brought needed financial support to many who thought college was an impossible dream. Even at institutions where TRIO programs were not present, institutionally supported programs were established to increase the diversity of the student body. The elements of the TRIO programs were emulated, including academic support, tutoring, special advising, mentoring, and programming. While both types of programs enriched the lives of many participants, they also created special centers and programs that isolated some students from the mainstream of campus life.

The Quest for Belonging and Equality

The Civil Rights movement and resulting federal legislation (Civil Rights Act of 1964) combined with increased diversity in immigrant populations literally has changed the face of American higher education. Many minority students came to campuses where they felt isolated and sought both academic and social support. A cluster of identity centers (Renn, 2011) were developed on many college campuses. Often real communities were formed with both academic and non-academic concerns being addressed by faculty, staff, and graduate and undergraduate students. Courses were developed, new majors and minors were introduced, and social networks were formed. First were centers and programs serving African American students and interests, including academic departments focused on African American Studies.

Centers for women students grew in the 1960s through the 1990s and provided both social and academic support for women, who enrolled in higher education in greater numbers than ever before. Academic departments focused on Women Studies were established and on some campuses changed over time into a focus on Gender Studies. The women's movement profoundly influenced higher education as women sought greater representation in many professions, including medicine and law.

Starting on the West Coast, centers focused on Latina/Latino interests were established with both academic and non-academic focuses. LGBT programs and centers soon followed on many campuses, and most recently Asian American and Native or Indigenous People Centers were developed. Renn states such centers and programs developed and were institutionally supported for four main reasons: responding to non-inclusive campus climates, supporting the ecology of the group involved, providing a bridge to close the organizational gap between student and academic affairs, and providing a place where traditions of the culture can be carried on and thus also have a symbolic function (Renn, 2011).

On some campuses, however, the establishments of specialized centers have at times been perceived by other students in negative ways by further isolating majority and minority cultures from one another on the campus. Others saw the need for a place to belong and flourish on a majority campus. Both perspectives are valid and must be considered as student affairs professionals address the question of advocating for some while supporting and advocating for all students.

Older Students

The average age of the American college student has risen in the last decade. This is due to several forces, including the economic downturn, the need for a work force with new skills and competencies, and the women's movement. The National Center for Educational Statistics (NCES) states that "In recent years, the percentage increase in the number of students age 25 and over has been larger than the percentage increase of younger students and the pattern is expected to increase" (NCES, 2010). In fact, NCES expects a 20 percent increase in older student enrollment in the next decade (NCES, 2012). Older students bring with them new and different issues to the collegiate environment, including balancing home and school responsibilities. Often older students enter higher education to gain specific skills and competencies to help them in a current employment situation or to aid them in preparing for a new career. As the economic base of the United States changes to meet new technological and environmental issues, the need for increased training and professional development is bound to grow and a greater number of older students are expected to enroll in colleges and universities.

A special subpopulation of older students are veterans returning to college after military service. Although many have earned financial support through their service, financing a college education remains a concern for veterans as it is for most returning students. Cost is often an issue and questions regarding mandatory fees, eligibility for financial aid, and child care are bound to increase rather than decrease as the student population ages. Some returning veterans also bring with them psychological issues that need to be addressed if they are going to thrive and succeed in the collegiate environment.

Older students are now an important part of many college campuses. New programs and services will need to be developed to directly address issues that may interfere with their potential academic success.

Changing Laws and Judicial Decisions

Brown v. Board of Education (1954) struck down the separate but equal doctrine in elementary and secondary education and has also had a lasting impact on the educational opportunities available to non-whites within higher education. While the times of active resistance to desegregation have abated, the issues of racism at worst and insensitivity at best are still present on many college campuses. Affirmative action programs aimed at increasing diversity in the student body have also been recently challenged in the courts.

The most recent case, as of this writing, reaffirmed the Supreme Court's opinion that strict scrutiny was needed by the Fifth Circuit to determine whether the admissions process of the University of Texas at Austin meets this standard, and the case was remanded for reconsideration by the Fifth circuit, stating that "the Fifth Circuit must assess whether the University has offered sufficient evidence to prove that the admissions program is narrowly tailored to obtain the educational benefits of diversity" (*Fisher v. University of Texas et al.*, 570 U.S. [2013]). The question for all institutions of higher education that was not settled is whether affirmative action programs can meet the strict scrutiny standard of the court. Such deliberations may raise questions of the legitimacy of admissions processes, but the opinion also underscores the appropriateness of diversity as an educational benefit to all students. Without doubt this will pose new questions and concerns among students and their families that must be addressed by institutions and the student affairs professionals who work within them.

Access for Those with Disabilities

Section 504 of the Rehabilitation Act of 1973 prohibited discrimination on the basis of handicap for individuals who were otherwise qualified for admission to both public and independent institutions receiving federal aid. That act and the Americans with Disabilities Act of 1990 prohibit discrimination on the basis of disability in employment opportunities, public accommodation, and transportation, among others. Combined, these two acts require institutions to assure that programs are accessible regardless of handicap, whether visible or invisible. In addition, the institution must provide necessary support for students to access educational opportunities if they are disabled. In combination, these acts have opened the doors of educational opportunities to many who would never have considered higher education, continuing education, or participation in the cultural life of the campus before. They also have brought with them enormous costs to institutions and situations where accommodations for some may inconvenience or interfere with the educational opportunities of others.

In addition, the hidden learning disabilities or mental health disabilities provide specific challenges for administrators who must balance the right to access with the need to have a safe learning environment for all students. For example, a student who is bipolar but is controlled regarding behavior by the use of prescribed medication may decide to not take medications anymore. His or her behavior and resulting incidents, including emergency admissions to the hospital, cause not only distress to self but to other students who are friends and classmates. Balancing those competing needs is one of the unintended consequences of this legislation, which pose enormous challenges for college student affairs administrators.

To fully understand the current issues on campus, student affairs professionals need to understand the history of how their institution became more diverse. What were the important events, people, and issues that brought diversity to the forefront at their specific institution? Each institution has a history with diversity, and understanding that history assists in understanding and confronting the current issues on campus.

While broad forces have changed the face of American higher education and a specific institution, the challenge in the current environment is to assure that all students have an equal opportunity to learn, grow, and thrive within an increasingly diverse community. The challenges are many as individuals with different backgrounds and life stories try to live, work, learn, and socially interact on college and university campuses. Often issues are presented as dichotomies: "If you do this for them why not for us?" or "Why do they need special treatment and support?" One of the biggest challenges facing student affairs professionals is that of achieving balance in our professional practice by serving all when we are supporting some in their educational goals on campus.

What Strategies Can Assist in Dealing with Diversity?

Diversity brings with it a number of educational and social challenges on the contemporary college campus. Students come to

college with a range of diversity experiences from broad inter-
cultural and interracial friendships and interaction to relative
isolation from others who are different from them.

Other chapters in this volume illustrate how the foundational
documents, theories, research, and professional literature of our
profession can assist practitioners in their daily work. All of these
sources can provide useful perspectives as strategies are developed to
build a diverse community in a collegiate setting. One size certainly
does not fit all when it comes to helping students encounter and
effectively deal with differences.

Creating Academic and Program Requirements Regarding Diversity

Visiting a college cafeteria on the contemporary college campus
illustrates the friendship gaps that often occur between students of
different cultural and ethnic backgrounds. Students tend to eat with
their friends, and often those friendships do not extend across
cultural, religious, and racial lines. However, for success after
college, it is important that students learn to close that gap while
they are in college for the likelihood that they will work with, be
supervised by, or supervise someone who is different from them in
some important dimension of their lives is very strong. To counter-
act the separation that occurs, many institutions have incorporated
diversity requirements as part of the curriculum and also included
exposure to diversity issues in the institutional orientation program.
It is unclear whether or not such requirements help close the gap,
and more research is needed in this important area.

Sharing Research Results and Information with Others on Campus

One strategy that is helpful in serving all students is to share what
student affairs knows about students with other parts of the academic community. For example, many institutions have participated in the Cooperative Institutional Research Program (CIRP)

for twenty or more years. Surveys of the attitudes and experiences of entering students are collected each year and changes in the entering freshman class can be noted for others in the institution. At one institution, a one-page summary of the most relevant parts of the CIRP data is sent to faculty along with a comparison on some of the variables to the entering freshman class of ten and twenty years ago. This report is a joint effort of the Division of Student Affairs and the Center for Teaching Excellence on the campus, and feedback from faculty has been very positive. As one faculty member put it, "I knew they had changed but I did not know how much!" The value of this report according to the faculty who receive it is that it helps them understand the differences in the student body that occur each and every year. Chapter 2 in this volume also provides more information on the use of data and research to inform, instruct, and assist the campus community.

Another general source that provides a perspective on how students have changed that is helpful to faculty colleagues is the Beloit College Mindset List, which can be found online and helps us all understand what the entering traditionally aged freshman class has experienced in their lifetime. Faculty members have found this list to be particularly useful as they try to provide analogies for traditionally aged students that have meaning for them.

Finally, research done by the division of student affairs on issues of student satisfaction, when shared across the institution, can be an instrument for change. At one institution, for example, a survey of student satisfaction indicated that Asian American students did not feel as strong a connection with faculty as did other groups of students, including African American and Hispanic/Latino students. The Division of Student Affairs planned and implemented a series of focus groups for students to try to pinpoint the reasons for dissatisfaction with faculty relations by Asian American students although they were, as a group, doing very well in courses. One finding that came out of the focus groups is that Asian American students and international students were not called on during discussions by name as frequently as other students. Several students said that they thought the faculty were concerned that they were going to mispronounce their name so chose not to call them by name. The researchers then met with faculty members across disciplines, who validated that perception. The result of this research was that the Teaching Center on campus employed native speakers who were available at the beginning of each semester to help faculty learn how to pronounce the names of all their students. Many faculty members took advantage of the help and began to feel more comfortable calling on all students by name, including Asian American and international students. When the study was repeated five years later Asian American students showed no statistical difference in their relationships with faculty than any other group of students. Sometimes answers to questions are easy to implement at relatively low cost.

Service Learning Opportunities

Development of community service programs also helps fill the friendship gap between disparate groups of students on campus. Working together on a project to help others is another way to highlight common concerns and interests (Jacoby, 1996). At some institutions these have been constituted as a service day for the entire institution, including faculty and staff. On other campuses the focus has been on projects in neighborhoods bordering the institution. On still other campuses the focus has been on year-long programs focused on helping students from grade school and high school master new skills both in the classroom and on the playing field. Through a year-long program connections are made between the college students and community students being helped. In addition, sustained contact by groups of students focusing on a common issue that needs to be addressed builds strong working relationships among the helpers, as well as those being helped.

Many academic classes are offering service learning opportunities as part of the curriculum. Often this provides another way for student affairs to support the academic mission of the institution by sharing connections with agencies and opportunities for service in the local community with faculty members interested in such learning opportunities. Helping identify possible placements for students for both short-term and long-term service can be a key role for student affairs with their academic partners. Such ventures, however, require sustained commitment on the part of the student affairs staff to maintain the connections and support for interested faculty.

Developing Connections across the Campus

Finally, honing skills focused on the development of connections across the campus to better serve students has never been more important. Understanding the complex organizational relationships on a college campus is never easy but can result in programs that help students learn and succeed in new and different ways. On one campus, new faculty are welcomed to campus with a personal note from a student affairs staff member who includes a small packet that focuses on how student affairs offices can be helpful to faculty. It contains specific references to issues such as organizing out-of-class learning experiences, dealing with disruptive students, seeking support for a student experiencing difficulty, and so forth. On another campus each new faculty member is given guest passes to eat in the dining halls as guests of the division. On still another campus the counseling center has developed a program of having assigned liaisons for each school or college, and those individuals meet regularly with the academic advising staff to pinpoint problems and work on making the referral process for students needing psychological help easier. Each campus will have to assess the climate on campus and identify the unique ways connections can help students grow, learn, and prosper.

Reaching out to faculty and providing information to help them deal with issues of concern are always useful strategies. The result on many campuses have been joint programs such as residential colleges with faculty masters, the development of freshman seminars on relevant topics of the day, tutoring services, writing centers, and other academic support programs that strengthen the experiences of all students.

Changing the Debate

The debate regarding diversity on campuses often comes down to decisions about the use of scarce resources. Decisions about whether or not to fund new initiatives is seen by some in the academic community as one of taking resources away from already established programs to fund something new. It is not always the case that one area has to give something up in order for something new to begin. Discussions about pooling scarce resources to fund new programs are usually helpful. Explaining what will *not* happen if the new approach is not funded is also useful and helps clarify the purposes of the proposed program. Arranging for those likely to be influenced and served by the new idea to have an opportunity to discuss their needs directly with decision makers in a non-confrontational manner can be very useful.

Looking at systems and structures rather than dwelling on people and personalities, Tierney (1999) urges institutions to look at how we serve our students and other constituents rather than focusing on our internal structures in higher education. He urges us to create conditions where those we serve can speak for themselves and really be heard. His perspective is valuable and worth considering as we try to build diverse campus communities.

On one campus, for example, students were concerned that they were not actively involved in the budget allocation process at the institution. The vice president for finance and the vice president for student affairs discussed the issue of active student involvement in the budget process. Together they developed a proposal to the president and the institutional budget committee to establish an Undergraduate Budget Priorities Committee. This committee, composed of students who applied for the committee and were chosen by the student government, was charged with responsibility of presenting requests for funding for the most important programs and activities for students. It was initially agreed that the institution would try this approach for one year. The students made a formal presentation to the budget committee and outlined their priorities for funding just as any unit of the institution would do. They did such an outstanding job that the committee became a formal part of the budgeting process. The students certainly did not "get" everything they asked for but gave such compelling arguments that they were funded for many of their priority projects. Student affairs staff initially worked with the students to prepare them for the process, but after a few years the students took responsibility for preparation of their own student committee. By taking a new and positive approach to student discontent a new vital part of the budget cycle became part of a transformative change in the budget process. A number of the proposals brought forward by the students and funded focused on community building and service learning—both proven strategies for building connections among students.

The cases presented in the next section focus on many of the issues student affairs professionals regularly encounter in their work. They provide unique opportunities for change to occur in institutional systems and in the people involved in the issue.

Case Studies

The following cases illustrate how student affairs professionals can use their knowledge and skills to help students and others in the community constructively confront situations when some students feel others are getting special treatment and other students believe that their unique differences and needs are not being recognized and accommodated by the institution.

Fairness in Fees

Omega University, a public institution, in a midwestern state has tuition costs set by the legislature. With the economic conditions in the state on the decline, the legislature limited tuition increases over the last ten years. While popular with the voters, the lack of resources caused Omega to lose some outstanding faculty and not be able to expand their facilities to meet a growing enrollment. At the time, Omega housed about 80 percent of the undergraduate student enrollment and the rest commuted from home or lived off campus.

The undergraduate students had been interested for some time in having the university construct and staff a new recreation and fitness center and pledged support for the sale of bonds through imposition of a new fitness fee for all full-time students, both graduate and undergraduate. Full-time status, in the student referendum, was defined as a student taking twelve semester hours or more. A vast majority of the traditionally aged undergraduate students supported the referendum, and it passed.

Very few students who were older than average voted in the referendum, and many of these students claimed they did not even know that the referendum was taking place. Graduate students were not specifically polled by the undergraduate student government. When the results of the referendum were made public, a group of older than average students made an appointment with the vice president for student affairs. They wanted to express their opposition to the new fee and discussed in detail the implications it had for those who had families and commuted to campus only when required to do so to attend classes. They indicated that they felt so strongly about the issue that they were prepared to engage in demonstrations against the new fee if it was on the agenda at the next governing board meeting. The vice president listened carefully to their position on the issue and indicated she would continue to talk with them before making a decision to ask the president to take the referendum to the board.

She informed the student government of the opposition to the imposition of the new fee by this group of older students and urged the student leaders to meet with the older student group to fully understand their views. They did so and were surprised to learn that almost 20 percent of the undergraduate student population was over twenty-five and that many of them carried full academic loads while working full-time. She urged the students to examine alternatives to a mandatory fee for all students that would accomplish their goal of a new recreation and fitness center. The student leaders asked that the presentation to the board be postponed until they could really examine the situation and the issues presented by the older students. The president and the vice president for student affairs agreed and also agreed to attend a number of open forums held not only on campus but also by video chat, which would permit more participation by older students. Both groups of students agreed and worked on several proposals that could be resubmitted to a referendum. The needs and wants of both groups of students were considered, and alternatives were presented for discussion at the forums. After several months of discussion the students agreed to submit three options to be considered by both graduate and undergraduate students.

1. The original referendum of a required fee for all students both graduate and undergraduate taking twelve semester hours or more.

2. A referendum of a required fee for all full-time undergraduate students taking twelve hours or more and an optional free for graduate students who would like to use the new recreation facility when it opened. An optional fee for the facility would also be available for faculty and staff.

3. A referendum for a required fee for all residential students regardless of graduate or undergraduate status and an optional fee for other students who would like to use the facility when

it opened. An optional fee for the facility would also be available for faculty and staff.

With support from both the undergraduate student government and the older student group, other organizations on campus were asked for their advice and input. As a result, the residence hall council, the ethnic student groups, the Greek organizations, the faculty senate, the professional staff council, the student government senate, and the graduate student council all supported the proposed compromise and the third option was overwhelmingly supported by the students.

The modified proposal was presented to the board that approved the sale of bonds based on the strong support of residential students for the required fee and the estimates for user fee income. Three years after the first referendum was conducted, bids were let and construction began on the new recreation facility.

Discussion. Taking time to listen to all sides, helping students clarify issues and understand the reasons behind opposition, and opening up dialogue between the concerned parties served the institution well. A balanced approach to the issue was developed that was fiscally sound and met the needs of the entire community. The undergraduate student leadership learned some important lessons on building coalitions and serving all students, and the older students felt that their legitimate concerns were recognized and supported.

Class Disruption

An entering freshman student came to the Disability office during the summer orientation program. He and his parents wanted to be assured that he would not be discriminated against because he had Tourette's syndrome. The staff member asked how his Tourette's syndrome manifested itself, and the student told of tics that caused him to verbalize loudly, which sometimes annoyed students around him in high school. His parents indicated that he was on a new medication and had not had any incidents this summer. They noted, however, that his summer had been stress free and he was not in any formal classes. The staff member urged the new student to come in when he had his schedule and they would work out a strategy for notification of his issues to his faculty members in the fall semester.

The new student came back to the office just after he moved into the residence hall. He seemed happy and relaxed and liked his new living situation. He asked that his faculty members be informed of his disability and promised that he would also go and talk to each faculty member early in the semester. He indicated in this meeting that his tics became more pronounced when he was under stress and he hoped that would not occur this year. During the conversation he told the staff member that his parents were very supportive and helpful. He asked the staff member to share information with them when they called and said he did not have a concern about involving his parents. At the close of the session the staff member discussed some relaxation exercises that might help him and urged him to get involved in some type of regular exercise program to cope with any stress that might occur.

Everything seemed to be going well in all classes but one. He often experienced loud verbal tics in American History class. These tics interrupted both lectures and presentations by other students. Several students had expressed their concern about his classroom behavior to the faculty member and the faculty member called the Disability office. The staff member who originally worked with the student called the student and asked him to stop by. She indicated to him that other students had found him to be disruptive in class and that his involuntary tics were interfering with their ability to learn. The student got very defensive and angry and said that his tics occurred only once in a while and usually did not last long. The staff member urged him to talk to the faculty member and then asked him what he thought would be the best solution to the issue of disruption in the classroom. He said he would work on calming down before class and hoped that would be the end of it.

It was not. At the end of the sixth week of classes his interruptions became more frequent and more complaints were made to the professor. His parents called and said that the institution was not making a reasonable accommodation for his disability. Because the staff member had explicit permission from the student he talked to them and frankly told them that his disruptions were becoming louder and more frequent and were interfering with the learning of other students. He was not having issues in any of his other classes but this particular class with the requirement for oral presentations seemed to make him quite anxious. He closed the conversation with the parents by assuring them that the institution also wanted their son to succeed and he would follow through with the student.

The staff member set up a meeting with the student and asked him what solutions he could see for the problem. He said he did not want to bother other students but was required to take this history class for his major. He felt badly but did not know what to do. The staff member suggested that there was another solution other than sticking it out in the class. He could be assigned to a private tutorial with a graduate assistant in the department. That might help him learn the material without having the stress of class presentations. The faculty member was amenable to that solution and so was the student. The parents were less enthusiastic, but they said that their son was extremely anxious and did not like to be the center of attention in the class. The tutorial was established. He completed the course through the tutorial and the other students returned to a non-disruptive classroom.

Discussion. The staff member involved did three important things. He listened to all the parties concerned with the issue. He then focused on what was best for the student with the disability and listened to his feelings. At no time did he promise that accommodations would be trouble free. He then developed a reasonable solution to the issue that honored the need for the student with Tourette's to complete the course and honored the needs of the other students to have a less disruptive learning environment. At no time did the staff member dismiss concerns by anyone involved as unimportant and took the time to develop a reasonable alternative. In addition, with help from the staff member, the student decided that he needed to work on controlling his stress in settings where he would need to make presentations in class. Through the counseling center on campus he learned stress reduction techniques that helped him in other classes throughout his college career.

Insensitivity or Racial Bias?

The students who lived on one residence hall floor decided to watch a popular reality television show each week together. Most students on the floor participated and made comments about the behavior of the participants in the show. They spent time after the show was over discussing what happened and how they felt about it. This season the show had one character who consistently made comments about others on the show regarding their race or their sexual orientation. Other members of the cast would respond to those comments by laughter or calling the person a redneck. The students on the floor shouted back at the person but some laughed and thought the comments were funny. This behavior bothered some of the minority students on the floor, and they got together and decided they would not come to the viewing the next night it was shown.

When the resident assistant realized that they were missing she went looking for them and found them in a room discussing how insensitive the other members of the floor had been when hurtful comments were made by the members of the cast. She went back to the group from the floor and quietly observed their behavior. She really had not paid much attention before because the comments on the show were obviously so racist and homophobic that she thought everyone would see them for what they were. But she tried to listen as she imagined her residents were listening to the comments made by their floor mates. At the end of the show when the discussion started, one of the residents looked around and realized none of the minority students on the floor had been at the viewing. He inquired why that had happened. The resident assistant felt she could not speak for the group that was missing but said she was concerned that the reaction of the members of the floor to the insensitive comments made by the cast member might have made the missing residents uncomfortable.

The discussion that happened after her comment made her realize that she needed some help to resolve this issue before it got bigger and more divisive. She went to her hall director and brought the students who were uncomfortable with her. They were even more verbal with the hall director, saying they were tired of educating other people and that people should know better. They were obviously hurt and angry about the response of their floor mates to the racist and homophobic cast member. The hall director heard them out and then suggested that rather than keeping these feelings to themselves that they should express them to the other members of the floor.

The students were reluctant to do so, but after talking it over with each other they said they would try but only if the hall director was there. She suggested that they also have someone come to the meeting with the other floor residents from the multicultural center. One of the staff members there was a good friend and had confronted such issues before. The students agreed, and the community assistant called a required floor meeting two hours before the regular time to view the television show.

The students all came, some complaining that the required meeting disrupted their planned study time. The hall director introduced herself and the staff member from the multicultural center. She said some of the students on the floor were uncomfortable about how some hall residents responded to the racist and homophobic comments made by the cast member. Immediately several students spoke up, making comments such as "We didn't mean anything by it." "We were just fooling around." "Why are you making such a big deal of something that was just done in fun?" It was then that the multicultural staff member spoke and said, "It is what we do thoughtlessly that hurts the most," and talked about an incident in his own life when he was in college and he made fun of a gay man. The man in question came up to him after that incident and told him how hurt he was because he thought he was my friend. "I tried to tell him I was just fooling around but he would not permit me to get away with that." He indicated that he and his former friend rarely spoke after that incident.

There was silence in the group and then one of the minority students spoke up, telling his floor mates how their comments made him feel. Then each of the students who had boycotted the last television watching session spoke up. It was quiet in the room and students were asked to examine what they had said and how it might hurt others. The conversation continued for some time and then it was time for the show to start. One of the members of the floor suggested that they record the show and stop the live performance when someone in the group who was not a minority heard a racist or homophobic comment by a member of the cast. That protocol was agreed on and the group proceeded to watch the show—watching not only the person making the offensive comments but the reaction of the other cast members.

They ended up not seeing much of the show but really understanding how actions and reactions can hurt other people. After this evening the whole floor decided this show wasn't as much fun as they thought it was and decided they could use their group time together to have more actual fun together. Although stilted at first, the conversations on the floor became more open and honest and better interactions between and among all the students occurred.

Discussion. The resident assistant, the hall director, and the multicultural staff person all responded to the concerns of the minority students. The choice of the multicultural staff person to share an incident from his own life helped the students understand that comments made in jest were not always perceived as funny and could be perceived as hurtful. Taking the time to confront the issues involved validated the minority students' concerns and also helped other residents really hear what they were saying. In addition, they learned that they need to listen to feedback and not assume that others see humor in the same way that they do. Firm friendships were not always the result but at a minimum the students on this floor understood that comments can wound even when you believe you are just fooling around. The vast majority of the floor residents indicated, at the end of the year, that this incident was important in increasing their understanding of others. It was an important lesson for all and illustrated the investment of time and energy that is necessary to create conditions where students can talk openly about issues of race and sexual orientation.

Do They Really Need That Space?

A private institution with a nominal protestant religious affiliation saw their undergraduate student body become increasing diverse in terms of ethnicity, race, sexual orientation, age, and religion. The institution has a university chaplain who has worked very hard to accommodate the religious diversity with the community. There is an interfaith student committee that meets regularly to discuss programs and activities where members of all religious groups can come together to work on projects of mutual interest and concern. Encouragement of diversity has been a key element in the development of the strategic plan for the institution, including the recruitment of international students.

A group of Muslim students approached the chaplain to ask that room be set aside for their use for daily prayers, which observant Muslims must make five times a day. They indicated that all of the Muslim students on campus were not observant but that some were. The leadership of the student group felt that the institution should accommodate this reasonable request.

Dedicated space on the campus, however, was at a premium. Student groups shared office space, and the chapel on campus was non-denominational. Some other student religious groups had asked that quiet mediation space be set up on campus for all students who practiced meditation. This request had also not been responded to by the administration. The Muslim students were persistent and started a letter-writing campaign to the president and other university officials. The president told the vice president for student affairs to do something about the situation.

The vice president called a staff meeting to respond to the request. The maintenance staff wanted to know who would clean the space. The security staff wanted to know who would open and close the room and how would they know if the proper people were using it. The chaplain was concerned that he had not been able to respond to reasonable space requests from other student religious groups whereas this request appeared to be getting high priority from the president and others in the institution. Other directors in the division of student affairs reminded the vice president that their requests for additional designated space had not been granted. No one appeared to be happy, but a solution needed to be found.

As a result of the meeting the vice president circulated a list of issues and problems associated with the request for dedicated prayer space. It was clear that no one at the meeting knew the size space the students were envisioning. In addition, it was not clear where on campus the students thought the space should be located, let alone who would clean the space and provide security or what the hours should be if space became available. At this point the chaplain became defensive, telling the vice president that he did not want to encourage the students by asking for a specific proposal that probably would not be granted.

The vice president calmly listened to the chaplain and told him that no one was accusing him of not taking the students seriously. The chaplain calmed down and began to talk about available spaces that he had been thinking about. The vice president suggested that he meet with the students and get them to answer the questions that came up at the meeting. Further, the vice president suggested that the students develop a specific proposal with the chaplain and then have it forwarded to his office. The chaplain was still uneasy and was concerned about leading the students down the "primrose path" but agreed to this approach with one caveat. He asked that the Muslim students have a discussion about their request with the Interfaith group he had established. The vice president agreed to this stipulation.

The Muslim students prepared a proposal with specific requests for the size of the room and the general location on campus. They agreed that they would take responsibility for cleaning the space but that once a week the cleaning staff would come in for a real cleaning after prayers were concluded for the day. The room would be locked at the end of the last prayer session of the day and someone from the Muslim student group would take responsibility for opening and closing the room. The space they were requesting was surprisingly small and they gave two or three alternatives for a location. The representatives of the Muslim Student Association agreed to discuss their proposal with the Interfaith group. At this discussion, concern was expressed that the university had not yet responded to the request from the Interfaith group for a quiet meditation space. The students worked together to modify the request for prayer space to include a modest proposal for an interfaith meditation space in one of the locations suggested by the Muslim student group. The proposal was sent to the vice president.

In the meantime, the president had been getting calls and letters from parents and alumni—some for and some against having dedicated space for Muslim students to pray. He discussed the issue with his cabinet and decided that the students had come up with a reasonable proposal and approved the dedication of the space granting use for one space for prayer and the other for meditation.

Discussion. By taking the time to involve both the students directly involved with the request and the Interfaith group in both discussing and eventually joining together to request both types of space, the chaplain and the vice president really listened to the students. They also let the students know about the legitimate concerns of others in the community and helped them develop solutions to those concerns. Respectful dialogue was initiated, and although some of the directors in the Division of Student Affairs felt that their own legitimate requests for additional space became a lower priority because of this student request, everyone agreed that the student request was legitimate and that it was consistent with the mission and goals of the institution.

The vice president then asked the directors in student affairs to prioritize their space requests just as the institution had asked the students to do. This brought about an honest and frank discussion by the directors of space and program needs, and some creative thinking emerged from those discussions. Although space remained an issue, progress was made in understanding the needs of others instead of just focusing on the needs of each department. A more unified voice began to be heard from the Division of Student Affairs about needs and concerns that needed to be addressed. As one director said, "We can always learn something from the students." And truer words were never spoken.

These four cases deliberately focused on small incidents and conflicts that had the potential to grow into bigger political and personal issues on the campus if they were not handled effectively. Using the skills and knowledge base that they had, these Student Affairs professionals were able to openly confront issues and help students come to understandings that probably would not have occurred if the incidents were ignored or brushed off. Solving problems are everyday issues in the professional life of Student Affairs administrators. By applying what they learned from their foundational documents and listening carefully to those around them, they served both their institutions and their students well.

Conclusion

As we try to create communities of learning on our college campuses we need to recognize that part of our task is helping students learn from encountering differences. We are all different in some important way, and recognizing those differences and advocating for groups with voices that may not be heard is part of our role as student affairs professionals. At the same time we are responsible for serving all the students on campus. By using theory, literature, research, and data as lenses to examine problems and issues, the participants in these cases made a difference.

Each year what seem like new problems come up on any college campus. Taking a moment to reflect and see what is the same and what can be learned from the past that can help us in the present can and does make a positive difference as new problems and issues emerge. Years ago Arturo Madrid wrote about being the *other* in a majority culture in education (1988). We have all been the other at some time in our life and need to remember how that feels as we experience a changing student body. That may be the best service any professional can give to their students and their institutions.

Reflective Questions

1. Would you have approached any of these cases differently than was done in the case studies?

2. What resources are available to you to help deal with problems between students related to race, ethnicity, sexual orientation, age, or other differences? Can you name them?

3. What other connections could you make to increase the voice of underrepresented students?

4. Have you shared any of the foundational documents in student affairs with decision makers on campus so that they understand your assumptions and beliefs? Why, or why not?

5. What issues related to difference do you see emerging on your own campus?

6. Have you done your "homework" regarding the history of diversity on your campus? Has that helped or hindered you in your quest to serve all students?

6

Fulfilling Our Responsibilities
as Educators

A strong argument can be made that human learning and development is at the center of all three important activities of any university or college—teaching, service, and research. It has long been recognized in higher education that learning and development by college students can be fostered by both the formal curriculum and the cocurriculum, and best learning environments are those in which thoughtful consideration is given to coordinating the learning objectives and opportunities in both environments (Kuh, 1996). Hence, one of the ways in which we in student affairs can lead necessary change in our institutions is by fulfilling our responsibility as educators.

This chapter addresses how student affairs professionals can construct their professional practice as centered on teaching and learning, and, in the course of so doing, address the challenges and opportunities that arise from daily professional practice in our field. First, teaching and learning are situated in the historical and contemporary context of student affairs professional practice. Then we describe what good teaching and learning looks like in student affairs with regard to the learning and development of individuals. Next, attention turns to the learning and development of organizations. Fulfilling our roles as educators requires a set of knowledge and skills, and those competences are reviewed in the chapter. We also review the concept of "teachable moments" as it relates to teaching and learning in student affairs. Case studies, drawn from institutions around the country, follow and illustrate the ways in which ideas about teaching can inform change leadership. The chapter closes with reflection questions.

Our hope is that this chapter is helpful in encouraging student affairs professionals to consider the ways in which framing their practice as a matter of teaching and learning can be helpful in leading change on their campus. *Student Affairs Staff as Teachers* (Moore, 2007), a monograph in the New Directions for Student Services series, serves as an excellent resource for those interested in such an effort. It is loaded with useful information and practical examples. In addition to pointing to the work of Moore and colleagues, we offer several specific recommendations intended to assist colleagues in enhancing their student affairs practice through a focus on teaching and learning.

Teaching and Learning in Historical and Contemporary Contexts of Student Affairs

From the earliest days of the field, truly powerful student affairs work has reflected the centrality of learning in our work. *The Student Personnel Point of View* (American Council on Education, 1949), one of the seminal documents in the history of student affairs, argues for a clear and concise definition of student affairs as teaching and learning, "The student personnel point of view encompasses the student as a whole. The concept of education is broadened to include attention to the student's well-rounded development—physically, socially, emotionally and spiritually,—as well as intellectually" (p. 17).

More recently, Jane Fried (1995) and associates make the case for student affairs work as an act of teaching and learning. They further link the work to diversity and multiculturalism, observing that good practice requires recognition of the social contexts in which the teaching and learning is taking place and the social environments and experiences that shape the understanding of both student affairs practitioner and student.

Blimling and Whitt (1997) identify seven principles of effective professional practice in student affairs:

1. Engage students in active learning.
2. Help students develop coherent values and ethical standards.
3. Set and communicate high expectations for student learning.
4. Use systematic inquiry to improve student and institutional performance.
5. Use resources effectively to achieve institutional missions and goals.
6. Forge educational partnerships that advance student learning.
7. Build supportive and inclusive communities.

With four of the seven principles explicitly referencing learning and development and a fifth addressing assessment—an essential element of institutional or organizational learning, Blimling and Whitt clearly situate teaching and learning as an essential element of student affairs practice.

Several major reports issues over the past twenty years have called for a recentering of teaching and learning in student affairs, professional practice in particular and in higher education more broadly. Summing up this body of work, Baxter Magolda and Magolda (2011) write,

> Collectively, these reports [*Student Learning Imperative*, *Powerful Partnerships*, *Learning Reconsidered*] call upon student affairs educators to carefully select knowledge relevant to context and bring this knowledge to the foreground of their consciousness for their day-to-day practice. Adopting learning as our central mission and the integration of student and academic affairs as essential ingredients of higher education, we underscore the

SLI's calls for student affairs educators to be experts on students, their environments, and the teaching and learning process, and we add to that list becoming an expert on oneself as a teacher and learner. (p. 5)

Sandeen (2004), writing in an issue of *Change* magazine focusing on education outside of the classroom, points to growth in programs of that type. He includes examples such as peer-based learning, service learning, and learning communities. Sandeen notes that student affairs professional are, or at least are able to be, significantly involved in such programs.

Blake (2007), addressing a contemporary issue that drives much of the current discourse in higher education, directly addresses the link between student affairs' role as educators and student success as measured by retention and persistence to graduation. "Although many colleges place considerable emphasis on attractive residences, technology, athletic facilities, and cocurricular programs in recruiting new students, the evidence is clear that ultimate success in retention to graduation requires increased emphasis on academic achievement through active student involvement in the learning process" (p. 65).

What Learning Looks Like

Developing a sense of what constitutes fulfilling our role as educators requires that we have a working definition of learning. In *Learning Reconsidered* (Keeling, 2004), learning is defined as

. . . a comprehensive, holistic, transformative activity that integrates academic learning and student development, processes that have often been considered separate, and even independent of each other. When we say learning, then, we do not mean exclusively or primarily academic instruction, the acquisition of disciplinary content, or classroom learning—though the rich definition

of learning we use certainly incorporates and includes all
of those things. We do not say learning and development
because we do not want to suggest that learning and
student development are fundamentally different things,
or that one does, or could, occur without the other. Nor do
we specify separate, distinct, or categorical learning (in the
pure academic sense) and developmental objectives and
outcomes. (p. 2)

We find this to be a particularly fulsome and helpful definition.
However, we are not fully aligned with the thoughts of Keeling and
colleagues with regard to nomenclature. The common pairing of
"learning" and "development" does not in our minds imply that one
can occur without the other, and so we have used the pair
throughout this chapter.   L +] together!

Powerful Partnerships: A Shared Responsibility for Learning (American
Association for Higher Education, American College Personnel
Association, and National Association of Student Personnel Administrators, 1998) offers a more process-oriented description. The report
offers the following ten principles of what learning is and how to
strengthen it:

1. Learning is fundamentally about making and maintaining
   connections: biologically through neural networks; mentally
   among concepts, ideas, and meanings; and experientially
   through interaction between the mind and the environment, self and other, generality and context, deliberation
   and action.

2. Learning is enhanced by taking place in the context of a
   compelling situation that balances challenge and opportunity,
   stimulating and utilizing the brain's ability to conceptualize
   quickly and its capacity and need for contemplation and
   reflection upon experiences.

3. Learning is an active search for meaning by the learner—constructing knowledge rather than passively receiving it, shaping as well as being shaped by experiences.

4. Learning is developmental, a cumulative process involving the whole person, relating past and present, integrating the new with the old, starting from but transcending personal concerns and interests.

5. Learning is done by individuals who are intrinsically tied to others as social beings, interacting as competitors or collaborators, constraining or supporting the learning process, and able to enhance learning through cooperation and sharing.

6. Learning is strongly affected by the educational climate in which it takes place: the settings and surroundings, the influences of others, and the values accorded to the life of the mind and to learning achievements.

7. Learning requires frequent feedback if it is to be sustained, practice if it is to be nourished, and opportunities to use what has been learned.

8. Much learning takes place informally and incidentally, beyond explicit teaching or the classroom, in casual contacts with faculty and staff, peers, campus life, active social and community involvements, and unplanned but fertile and complex situations.

9. Learning is grounded in particular contexts and individual experiences, requiring effort to transfer specific knowledge and skills to other circumstances or to more general understandings and to unlearn personal views and approaches when confronted by new information.

10. Learning involves the ability of individuals to monitor their own learning, to understand how knowledge is acquired, to develop strategies for learning based on discerning their capacities and limitations, and to be aware of their own ways

of knowing in approaching new bodies of knowledge and disciplinary frameworks.

With a definition of learning in hand and a sense of what constitutes good learning, we turn our attention to developing an understanding of what good teaching looks like. Nevitt Sanford, who was for many years a professor in psychology at the University of California Berkeley, offers a stunningly simple but elegant model for consideration. Sanford (1962) argues that learning requires a balance of challenge and support. Hence, good teaching offers that balance. In subsequent work, Sanford (1966) added a student quality—readiness—to his model. The notion of challenge is closely related to the construct of cognitive dissonance, which is the sense of unease that results when a person encounters an unknown entity or idea. Teaching and learning is not optimized with either too much or too little dissonance (Atherton, 2013); as with Goldilocks, it has to be just right. Recently, George McClellan and his colleagues at Indiana University–Purdue University Fort Wayne (IPFW) have extended Sanford's work by adding celebration as an important element of teaching and learning. Examples of celebratory actions include, among a range of options, simple words of praise or congratulation, certificates or awards, or ceremonies. Such celebrations reinforce the individual effort of a particular student, encourage other students to achieve their own successes, and signal the importance of learning on campus. In addition to using the model to guide the way in which they shape programs and services, the student affairs professionals at IPFW explicitly draw on the work of Sanford in their professional and paraprofessional development programs, presentations to faculty members and academic advisors, and workshops for students.

Student affairs professionals interested in becoming good teachers might consider exploring the literature on the scholarship of teaching, a term that is generally used to refer to a movement in higher education to improve student learning through purposeful and scholarly study of teaching and learning. The Carnegie Foundation for the Advancement of Teaching argues that the movement "fosters significant, long-lasting learning for all students; enhances the practice and profession of teaching, and; brings to faculty members' work as teachers the recognition and reward afforded to other forms of scholarly work" (Carnegie Foundation for the Advancement of Teaching, 2013). Two seminal works, *Scholarship Reconsidered* (Boyer, 1990) and *Scholarship Assessed* (Glassick, Huber, and Maeroff, 1997), are valuable resources for student affairs professionals interested in the scholarship of teaching and learning.

Drawing on the work of Huber and Hutchings (2005) regarding how faculty engage in the scholarship of teaching and learning, Ribera, Fernandez, and Gray (2012) describe four stages through which faculty colleagues engaged in the scholarship of teaching and learning. Those stages are described in Table 6.1.

Table 6.1 Four Stages of Engagement in the Scholarship of Teaching and Learning

Stage	Activity
Develop specific questions about teaching and learning	Engage in systematic inquiry to understand student learning, both content and processes (Basis upon which scholarship of teaching and learning is built)
Gather and examine evidence of teaching and learning	Assess student learning and evaluate effectiveness of teaching
Try out new teaching practices and refine assessment methods	Refine teaching and learning
Disseminate scholarship in effort to foster best practices	Utilize publications and presentations to share process and findings (Obligation of professional practice)

Adapted from Ribera, Fernandez, and Gray (2012)

In addition to the literature on the scholarship of teaching and learning, Moore and Marsh (2007) identify several important strategies for student affairs professionals interested in success in improving their teaching skills. These include having a well-developed philosophy of teaching; creating a clear syllabus; evidencing professionalism, authority, and approachability; actively engaging students in their learning; and utilizing multiple forms of assessment and feedback.

The ways in which these strategies can be applied by student affairs professionals teaching in a formal course is obvious, and the ways in which almost all of these strategies can be adapted to teaching and learning outside the classroom is also fairly clear. However, one of those in-class ways deserves additional discussion as it relates to student affairs practitioners and teaching outside of the classroom. The typical syllabus for a course provides a student with information about the course (title, course number, section, etc.), the instructor (contact information and hours of availability), anticipated outcomes for the course, content that will be covered, time line for the course, and assessment (grading policies, attendance expectations, etc.). If we in student affairs understand and value the importance of a syllabus in a formal course, why would we not see the same value in a syllabus for learning experiences outside of a formal course? The authors believe that the development and distribution of a syllabus for student affairs programs and services could be a very useful device for helping student affairs professionals construct their work as teaching and learning, building connections with faculty colleagues, and providing a framework through which assessment data can be collected.

The syllabi for our programs and services could be shared in a variety of formats, depending on the particular circumstances and audiences for a given program or service. For example, the syllabi for an ongoing multifaceted program focused on fostering financial literacy might have a single unified syllabus for the full program posted online with information about the availability of the syllabus being included in all marketing materials for the program and at the program itself. A syllabus for a one-time program presenting a speaker on intellectual property rights and copyright law could be shared with those entering the program with assessment questions offered on the opposite side of the handout. A syllabi for a service indicating the outcomes the department hopes will be achieved during a visit could be provided using the website of the office providing the service or a sign posted in that office. For example, a housing department publicizing the upcoming lease renewal period could include on its renewal website information indicating that as a result of participating in the leasing process students will learn about contract law, rights and responsibilities of tenants, and decision making. The housing department could also indicate the outcomes they hope to achieve with regard to process participation and satisfaction in addition to explicitly sharing the intended learning outcomes. The office could note that they will be measuring progress toward the learning, participation, and satisfaction outcomes through survey instruments and other data sources. A particularly savvy housing operation could use appropriate technology to have students participate in online assessment of their learning with immediate feedback on how they fared, which would help reinforce the learning process.

Critical Theoretical Perspectives

To this point in the chapter, the information and ideas shared about teaching and learning come from a fairly traditional functionalist perspective. It is worth noting, however, that a great deal has been written in this area from a critical theoretical perspective.

In *The Power of Critical Theory: Liberating Adult Learning and Teaching*, Stephen Brookfield's outstanding resource on critical theoretical considerations in teaching and learning, he writes about the purposes of learning:

. . . critical theory is normatively grounded in a vision of a society in which people live collectively in ways that encourage the free exercise of their creativity without foreclosing that of others. In such a society people see their individual well-being as integrally bound up with that of the collective. They act toward each other with generosity and compassion and are ever alert to the presence of injustice, inequity, and oppression. Creating such a society can be understood as entailing a series of learning tasks: learning to recognize and challenge ideology that attempts to portray the exploitation of the many by the few as a natural state of affairs, learning to uncover and counter hegemony, learning to unmask power, learning to overcome alienation and thereby accept freedom, learning to pursue liberation, learning to reclaim reason, and learning to practice democracy. (2005, p. 39)

What does good teaching look like from a critical theoretical perspective? The work of hooks (1994) relating a personal narrative of teaching as transgressive, Giroux (1992) discussing teaching as border crossing in a post-9/11 world, or Freire (1970, 1994) arguing for teaching as an act of liberation all have something to offer to readers interested in work born of postmodern perspectives. While not works commonly featured in student affairs graduate preparation programs or professional development seminars, these and others written from the perspective of critical theory can be invaluable to those interested in the intersection of change and teaching and learning in higher education.

Learning Organizations

Our discussion of student affairs professionals as educators has to this point focused on teaching and learning as they relate to individuals, specifically as they relate to students. However, as Senge (2006) explains, organizations can learn too. As it relates to student affairs practice, organizations can include, among other things, student organizations, committees, administrative units, student affairs division, or the institution as a whole.

Senge describes a learning organization as a group working collectively to enhance their capacities to create results about which they care (Fulmer and Keys, 1998). Senge (2006) lists five disciplines found in a learning organization: systems thinking, personal mastery, mental models, shared vision, and team learning.

In describing the importance and process of organizational learning, Argyris (1999) notes organizations require current knowledge about new products and production processes, awareness of the environmental context in which they operate, and creation of innovative ways to utilize the knowledge and skills of all members of the organization. Developing and maintaining these characteristics necessitates cooperation across the organization, open and reliable communication, and trust. This sounds very much like the requirements and characteristics of a vibrant and transformative university community, and it is clear in our minds that student affairs professionals are well situated to play a vital role in assuring their institutions and their divisions of student affairs are truly learning organizations in the manner described by Senge (2006) and Argyris (1999).

Competencies of Teaching and Learning

The American College Personnel Association and the National Association of Student Personnel Administrators, the two largest general student affairs professional associations, cooperatively identify a set of core competencies required for the effective professional practice in the field (American College Personnel Association and National Association of Student Personnel Administrators, 2010a). Facilitating student learning and development is identified as one of these competencies. Specifically, "The Student Learning and Development competency area addresses the concepts and principles of student development and learning theory. This includes the ability to apply theory to improve and inform student affairs practice, as well as understanding teaching and training theory and practice" (p. 26).

There are a substantial number of resources available to student affairs professionals interested in developing their skills as teachers. Examples of such resources include campus-based faculty development programs that may be open to student affairs professionals, programs at professional conferences, and publications including articles in periodicals as well as monographs and books. In the interest of brevity, we will limit ourselves here to sharing two that we find particularly helpful and interesting.

One such resource was discussed earlier. Senge (2006) identifies personal mastery as one of the disciplines present in learning organization. His explanation of that discipline can be very helpful to a student affairs professional interested in developing as an educator. Senge describes personal mastery as a commitment to the process of learning. He notes that personal mastery comes about through an openness to learning, opportunities to learn, and practice.

Baxter Magolda's work on the ways in which student affairs professionals can support students in their development of self-authorship is another resource for those interested in strengthening their skills as a teacher. She defines self-authorship as "the internal capacity to define one's beliefs, identify, and social relations" (Baxter Magolda, 2008, p. 269) and identifies three elements of it: trusting the internal voice, building an internal foundation, and securing internal commitments. Referencing student affairs practitioners and other teachers and building on the work of Kegan (1994), Baxter Magolda (2012) states:

> Educators who take up the challenge of helping students become self-authoring must have gone through

this process themselves. They must be able to envision the growth required for success in adult life; articulate it in the form of learning goals; develop educational practices that effectively support and challenge students to make the necessary mental shifts; and act on this vision despite students', parents', or administrators' resistance to it.

An extensive literature exists on the pedagogy that helps learners construct their own increasingly complex perspectives, which has been variously called *liberatory*, *empowering*, *critical*, *feminist*, *culturally relevant*, and *constructivist*. Kegan (1994) described it as "a developmental bridge that welcomes learners' current meaning-making capacities (and thus provides support) and simultaneously invites them to move toward more complex capacities (and thus provides challenge)."

Baxter Magolda (2012) identifies a number of institutions as exemplars illustrating the ways in which student affairs professionals can engage in self-authorship as a means to being able to help students in their own self-authorship.

Purposefulness

Woven throughout Senge's (2006) discussion of personal mastery is a sense of the purposeful pursuit of improvement with regard to knowledge and skills. Purposefulness is also prominently addressed in *The Student Learning Imperative* (American College Personnel Association, 1996), which argues, "Student affairs professionals are educators who share responsibility with faculty, academic administrators, other staff, and students themselves for creating the conditions under which students are likely to expend time and energy in educationally-purposeful activities. They endorse talent development as the overarching goal of undergraduate education; that is, the college experience should raise students' aspirations and contribute to the development of skills and competencies that enable them to live productive, satisfying lives after college. Thus, student affairs programs and services must be designed and managed with specific student learning and personal development outcomes in mind." Clearly, purposefulness is a critically important element of any effort on the part of a student affairs professional to develop as a teacher and learner and to integrate that development into their professional practice.

In addition, as noted in *Powerful Partnerships: A Shared Responsibility for Learning* (American Association for Higher Education, American College Personnel Association, and National Association of Student Personnel Administrators, 1998):

> Despite American higher education's success at providing collegiate education for an unprecedented number of people, the vision of equipping all our students with learning deep enough to meet the challenges of the post-industrial age provides us with a powerful incentive to do our work better. People collaborate when the job they face is too big, is too urgent, or requires too much knowledge for one person or group to do alone. Marshaling what we know about learning and applying it to the education of our students is just such a job. This report makes the case that only when everyone on campus—particularly academic affairs and student affairs staff—shares the responsibility for student learning will we be able to make significant progress in improving it. (p. 1)

The faculty at many institutions have developed and approved a set of institutional learning outcomes. Rather than articulating a set of outcomes of their own, we recommend that student affairs professionals give serious thought to simply adopting the institutional learning outcomes as their own. Explicitly connecting student affairs programs and services to institutional learning out-comes, assessing the contribution of those programs and services to learning, and sharing findings from that assessment are all ways in which student affairs can develop and sustain strong partnerships with leaders in the faculty and academic administration.

The role of the faculty in controlling the curriculum in colleges and universities is an essential principle of shared governance in higher education, and that principle is reflected in the founding documents of our profession (see Chapter 1). Recognizing and respecting that role can provide an opportunity through which student affairs professionals can develop stronger relationships with faculty colleagues and strengthen recognition of their role as educators in the campus community.

This is not to say that student affairs ought to abandon the traditional or contemporary knowledge, skills, or attitudes that it seeks to foster in students. MacKinnon, Broido, and Wilson (2004) explain, "The teaching and learning domains of student affairs focus on knowledge, skills, and attitudes that evolve from the classic student affairs literature: cognitive competence, intrapersonal competence, interpersonal competence, content knowledge competence, and citizenship competence (Baxter Magolda, 1999; Light, 2001; MacKinnon-Slaney, 1994)" (p. 394). It is our observation that these domains lend themselves to association with the learning outcomes typically expressed in institutional learning outcome statements. For example, student affairs professionals often think of themselves as being in position to help students learn how to communicate with others, to engage in community service, or to conduct themselves ethically. All are knowledge, skills, or attitudes that are frequently embedded in institutional learning statements.

Teachable Moments

Having shared thoughts on what good teaching and learning look like for both individuals and organizations, as well as thoughts on the competencies required of a student affairs practitioner wishing to fulfill their role as educator, we turn our attention to the question of timing. When will all this teaching and learning take place?

Havighurst (1952, p. 7), in discussing human learning and development, writes, "A developmental task is a task which is learned at a specific point and which makes achievement of succeeding tasks possible. When the timing is right, the ability to learn a particular task will be possible. This is referred to as a teachable moment. It is important to keep in mind that unless the time is right, learning will not occur. Hence, it is important to repeat important points whenever possible so that when a student's teachable moment occurs, s/he can benefit from the knowledge."

We in student affairs often speak of challenging or unexpected situations as teachable moments. A student group invites a speaker with a history of statements that are viewed as hurtful or offensive by one or more campus communities. A freshman living away from home for the first time does not handle the freedom well, performs poorly in classes, and is placed on academic probation. A staff member mishandles publicity efforts for a program with the result being a very low turnout for a very costly event. Certainly these are all teachable moments in the way that the term is typically understood.

Note, however, that Havighurst's (1952) description of teachable moments does not necessarily require them to be unplanned or unexpected. The first advising appointment with a new student is certainly a teachable moment. The writing process for a student leader's presentation to the university's governing board is a teachable moment. A rising senior planning to search for employment or graduate education opportunities is a teachable moment. All are foreseeable, and student affairs professionals interested in fulfilling their role as educators are well positioned to support student learning and development at such times.

Our answer is simple and clear—every moment is a teachable moment. We concur with Dungy's (2004) observation that, "The pedagogy of student affairs uses the resources inherent in students' life experiences, along with the energy created by the conflict or challenge, to intentionally guide students to acquire knowledge through the active context of their lives."

Case Studies

Our purpose in sharing the following case studies is to illustrate the ways in which information shared in this chapter might be applied to everyday practice in student affairs. The recommendations are offered in the same spirit.

Big Deal University

Big Deal University (BDU) is a private, mid-sized, research intensive institution with a selective admissions policy. Its students are a diverse group drawn from across the country and around the world. While many are students from families with considerable means, a number come from families with modest to little financial resources. All have demonstrated great academic success in high school.

Student affairs at BDU employed a large number of student paraprofessional staff to help in offices and with various programs and services—resident assistants, peer health educators, peer academic advisors, orientation assistants, and others. The amount of time and energy invested in all the various training programs for the individual groups of paraprofessionals was substantial. The vice chancellor of student affairs wondered if there might be a better way to approach their training and asked the dean of students to pull a group together to study the division's paraprofessional training program.

The dean convened a committee that included the nine department heads from the units in student affairs that employ paraprofessionals. After getting nominations from those nine unit heads, the dean also invited three student paraprofessionals to join the working group.

At their first meeting, members of the committee discussed the various training programs in place. The purpose, goals, and methods of each of the programs were shared. Once all the data were gathered, the dean expressed it in a spreadsheet and shared the presentation with the committee. The members were invited to identify overarching themes or other commonalities. One of the student members, who held paraprofessional positions in two of the units, commented that there was considerable overlap in the content of the training with regard to several key concepts—diversity, respect for autonomy, ethical conduct, and confidentiality. Building on the student member's observation, the director of the Academic Support Center (who came to the position from the ranks of the BDU faculty) observed that, while the purpose of all the programs was to foster learning and development, no one had explicitly used that language in discussing their training programs. The director also noted that there did not seem to be a purposeful effort to express program outcomes in written form, share them with the paraprofessionals in training, or to assess whether or not those trainees are actually making progress with regard to the desired learning and development—all activities that would likely occur if the students were involved in learning opportunities in a course or other formal setting.

BDU had a strong College of Education, and a number of the faculty members there were engaged in collaborations of one sort or another with student affairs. The dean shared the committee's spreadsheet and subsequent conversation with two of those colleagues and invited them to come to the next meeting of the group with any thoughts or recommendations they might wish to share.

At that next meeting, the two faculty colleagues presented several ideas for consideration. One was to create a common course into which all student paraprofessionals could be enrolled. The course would

- Address the common core content identified through the committee's deliberations

- Be co-taught by a faculty colleague (who will receive additional travel funding into their own professional development funds in return for their efforts) and two BDU student affairs professionals (who will be chosen based on a number of factors, including their opportunity to learn from the experience)

- Have a syllabus, specified learning outcomes, and a robust assessment program

- Be based online on an ongoing basis and credit (pass) given for completion once there is evidence that the paraprofessional has attained all of the specified learning outcomes

The faculty members recommended that the course include opportunities for the paraprofessional trainees to reflect on the ways in which what is learned in the course can be used in their student positions, as well as in other areas of their life. They also suggested that the course should include a blend of readings, video content, and interactive assessments (with notes with helpful information that pop up when a student selects an incorrect answer). One of the faculty members, who was teaching an advanced course in curriculum design next term, offered to have his class take on the development of the paraprofessional training program as one of their projects.

The dean and the members of the committee completed their review and presented their proposal to the vice chancellor. They proposed that the common course be implemented, that students be required to complete it during their first term of employment in a student affairs position, that each of the units develop an in-house training program to help paraprofessionals gain the knowledge and skills specific to their role in that particular department, and that common program and local programs be linked in thoughtful and purposeful ways.

The vice chancellor gratefully accepted the recommendations of the working group. In addition to their suggestions, the vice chancellor arranged to provide the two student affairs professionals who took on responsibility for co-teaching the common course with an opportunity to attend conferences and workshops on campus and elsewhere that focused on the scholarship of teaching and learning.

Discussion. One group of students for whom student affairs professionals play a unique education role is the group of students who work in our offices as paraprofessional staff. Constructing their service as a learning opportunity with specific outcomes and assessing both the process and the outcomes are important ways in which we can fulfill our role as educators. This case provides an example of how one group of student affairs colleagues came to recognize and address this opportunity (see the work of Koch, 2012, for another).

The case also highlights the importance of purposefulness. The discussion regarding paraprofessional training at Big Deal University originates out of practical considerations regarding the prudent use of the resources of staff time and departmental funds. In reviewing utilization, the work group begins to map learning outcomes but does so without initially recognizing them as such. It is at the point the director of the Academic Success Center explicitly references the absence of purposeful mention of learning outcomes that the conversation and the program take a crucial turn.

Once the paraprofessional development program is recognized as focusing on learning outcomes, the committee moves to invite faculty colleagues into the process. This opens up opportunities to develop collaborative programming between student affairs and faculty colleagues, and it helps assure richer learning opportunities for paraprofessionals, professionals, and faculty members alike.

Fundamental Shift College

Despite a portfolio that included significant resources and responsibilities, student services at Fundamental Shift College (FSC) was historically largely overlooked or ignored in important campus conversations. While students appreciated and recognized the efforts of the staff in Student Services, the same was not true of colleagues in either administrative or academic roles across campus. There was an ambivalence about the organization and its contributions to the mission of FSC, and at times that ambivalence drifted toward antipathy when various Student Services' policies or procedures were seen as impeding (or at least not advancing) progress toward goals of interest to the faculty or others.

The dean of students, a long-time staff member at the small, private, coastal college, had recently retired. The president of FSC saw this as an opportunity to bring in a change agent as the leader of Student Services. The president hoped that with new leadership the programs and services offered through student services might be more closely aligned with the core enterprise of the college— helping prepare students for meaningful lives. Sharing that vision with leaders of the students, staff, and faculty of FSC, the president set ought to hire the next dean of students.

The person chosen for the position came to FSC with a firmly held belief that the work of student affairs professionals should first and foremost be about learning and development of the whole student. The new dean's first few weeks at FSC were spent in meetings with student, staff, and faculty leaders from across campus as well as in meetings with members of the student services staff. At each of these meetings the dean shared a vision for student services as a unit that can and should play an integral role in supporting the success of students and the institution through focusing its programs and services on student learning and development. The reaction from across campus was generally positive though a bit doubtful as to whether or not such a change could be pulled off. While a few of the staff in student services were very positive about the new vision, the reaction of many (if not most) was to wonder why there was a need to change something that was not seen by them as being broken. They were not so much resistant as uninformed and uncommitted.

The dean began the process of changing the culture of student services with several important decisions. The name of the division was changed to Student Development, and the dean began openly discussing the nature of the change that Student Development was undertaking and a general process and time line for bringing about that change. That process included three phases: professional development; implementation; and assessment, revision, and celebration.

A professional development program was created to help provide staff in the division with information about student learning and development. That program included participation by faculty colleagues as well as student affairs professionals from other institutions with an interest in the scholarship of teaching. There was a presentation on the history and philosophy of higher education so that staff members could place the change in emphasis within a historical and contemporary context. Cognitive theories and the latest information on learning and the brain were shared. Information on learning styles and learning technologies was offered, as was information on assessment of learning and development.

Once there was a sense that the Student Development staff had a shared baseline of information about teaching and learning, the dean asked the group to move into the implementation phase. The first step was to invite Student Development to situate its efforts related to teaching and learning within the efforts of the faculty at FSC. Toward this end, the dean invited the chair of the FSC Faculty Senate to come to a meeting of the Student Development leadership group to present on FSC's *Undergraduate*

Learning Outcomes, a statement approved a few years ago by the FSC Faculty Senate and endorsed by the institution's president. Following the chair's presentation, the dean encouraged those present (including the Senate chair) to talk about the ways in which the programs and services of Student Development could contribute toward student achievement in the various goals described in the document. It quickly became apparent that there were more opportunities at hand than some might have otherwise thought, and the Student Development staff participating in the meeting readily accepted the dean's recommendation that they adopt FSC's *Undergraduate Learning Outcomes* as a guiding document for their services and programs.

Following up, the dean of students invited the senior leadership to revisit the mission statement for Student Development. It was also announced that moving forward both individual annual performance evaluations and unit annual reports would substantially focus on the ways in which the individual professional or unit contributes to student and institutional success as described in the *Undergraduate Learning Outcomes*. The dean pledged to create a communication plan for campus, alumni, and others that would highlight the contributions of staff and units to student learning and development, and the dean also promised to continue to present information on teaching and learning as part of Student Development's professional development plan. Finally, with the support of FSC's president, it was announced that FSC would add a teaching award for those outside the faculty who make a significant contribution to student learning and development.

Discussion. That Fundamental Shift's new dean of students frames student affairs professional practice as teaching and learning is not an accident. The professional preparation path that the dean traveled before coming to his new role included exposure to this concept in his graduate preparation program, early professional experiences, and professional association activities. He had come to understand his own professional practice as teaching and learning, and he felt very comfortable in that identification and understanding.

Having arrived at Fundamental Shift, the dean of students constructs the necessary change as a teaching and learning process rather than as a management process. He signals the shift early and often, including an important and highly visible symbolic act in changing the name of the division. The dean's commitment of divisional resources, both time and funds, to professional development in the area of teaching and learning further emphasizes that change was in the wind.

The decision to adopt learning outcomes, and specifically to adopt the institutional outcomes approved by Fundamental Shift's faculty, and to invite faculty leadership into the discussion is pivotal in this case study. Those decisions, along with the institutionalization of those decisions through incorporation in assessment, planning, and celebration, are defining distinctions for the future of the division and for the way in which the division relates to institutional partners and institutional mission.

Southern States University

Southern States University (SSU) is a mid-sized public institution with a proud tradition. Among its many strengths was a robust Greek system, a highly successful intercollegiate athletics program, and Commanders—a large and active leadership program with a quasi-military structure. Unfortunately, with these strengths came challenges. One of those challenges was that these very visible elements of the campus community had a decidedly masculine bent to them, and among the ways in which masculinity was socially constructed at SSU (and elsewhere) was a positive relationship between drinking and being male and that males are strong and not particularly communicative when it comes to personal experiences. Among the ways in which these social constructions played themselves out at SSU was a troubling amount of alcohol abuse and very little open discussion (outside of posturing) about alcohol abuse.

A member of SSU's faculty lived next door to one of the Commanders, and that student opened up privately in the past to the faculty member regarding concerns about the behavior of some students related to alcohol and about the impact that such behavior had on other members of the campus community. In addition, the faculty member suspected over the years that poor performance in the classroom by some of their students may have been the result of their involvement with alcohol or with others whose behavior was influenced by alcohol.

The faculty member's daughter went to the same middle school as the daughter of SSU's health and wellness coordinator. One day as they both waited for their girls to emerge from school, the two began to talk about the alcohol culture on campus and its impact on student success. They both noted the role that notions of masculinity seemed to be playing in the problem. The health and wellness coordinator recalled an article they had read about a program at another college that was using theater as a means to engage men in conversations about intimacy and sexual responsibility. As the faculty member and the staff member continued their conversation, they began to flesh out the idea for a program that would provide opportunities for students (including male students) to use the arts to express their experiences, feelings, and insights regarding the use and misuse of alcohol.

The faculty member and the staff member agreed to co-facilitate a conversation involving faculty members and student affairs staff to give further thought to the possibility of creating such a program. The faculty member recruited colleagues in theater, music, visual arts, literature, and dance. The staff member recruited colleagues in student activities and student conduct, as well as students from student assembly (SSU's student government), peer health education, athletics, and the Commanders.

What came of the discussion was a proposal to create a program that would integrate in-classroom learning with out-of-the-classroom learning in an effort to facilitate student learning and development related to the impact that alcohol has on them, their campus, and their community. A primary principle of the program was that student voices had to be at the center of the project, and that those voices had to be heard without judgment or prejudice. A second principle was that everyone involved in the project—faculty members, students in classes, student affairs professionals and paraprofessionals, and audience members from both the campus and community—were teachers and learners.

Faculty members in each of the disciplines agreed to focus discussion and assignments in their classes on this topic. Students wrote one-act plays, choreographed dance pieces, created photographic exhibits or other visual pieces, or composed music as their term-long projects in various courses. These works were presented as part of the week-long series.

Student affairs professionals and paraprofessionals were invited to classes to participate in discussions of the works as they were developed. They helped students learn how to communicate in ways that opened discussion up rather than shut it down, how to recognize and respond to "humorous" comments that reflected nervousness or reluctance, and how to critically reflect on the stories that were being shared.

In addition to faculty's assessment of student learning in the context of the formal course and to self-assessment of all participants conducted through journaling about their experiences in creating and implementing the program, both faculty members and student affairs professionals collaborated to develop assessment instruments to be used with those who would attend one of the performances or visit one of the gallery exhibits during the week-long program. All members of the original planning group—students, faculty, and staff—participated in the post-program analysis of the data collected through the various assessments.

Feedback from all involved in the creation and presentation of the project was overwhelmingly positive, and the learning and development evidenced in the various assessments was remarkable.

Several of the faculty members submitted articles (some coauthored with student affairs professionals) on the project to publications interested in the scholarship of teaching. Perhaps most impressively, the students in the classrooms and in the audiences were excited by the program and pressed for it to become an annual event on campus.

Discussion. As noted in Chapter 1, some challenges seem to go on forever. Some challenges with which student affairs professionals deal certainly seem that way. The potential harm from students' use, misuse, or abuse of alcohol is one of those. While impossible to calculate with certainty, it is certain that the total costs of student affairs programming and services dedicated to this challenge is staggering, and yet the challenge that vexed the foremothers and forefathers of our field still vexes us today.

The case of Southern States University's program offers an example of a creative approach that incorporates creative expression as a vehicle for fostering learning. The program is constructed in a way that capitalizes on existing opportunities in the curriculum and emphasizes development of both student affairs professionals and faculty members as teachers in the course of engaging students in a rich learning experience.

Conclusion

Several times in this chapter we have drawn on *Powerful Partnerships: A Shared Responsibility for Learning* in supporting our line of discussion. Our having done so reflects our respect for the statement and our belief in the ideas it expresses. It should not be surprising that we draw on that source once again as we prepare to close this chapter on student affairs professionals fulfilling our role as educators.

> Collectively, we know a lot about learning. A host of
> faculty, staff, and institutional initiatives undertaken

since the mid-80s and supported by colleges and universities, foundations, government, and other funding sources have resulted in a stream of improvement efforts related to teaching, curriculum, assessment, and learning environments. The best practices from those innovations and reforms mirror what scholars from a variety of disciplines, from neurobiology to psychology, tell us about the nature of learning. Exemplary practices are also shaped by the participants' particular experiences as learners and educators, which is why a program cannot simply be adopted but must be adapted to a new environment.

Despite these examples, most colleges and universities do not use our collective wisdom as well as they should. To do so requires a commitment to and support for action that goes beyond the individual faculty or staff member. Distracted by other responsibilities and isolated from others from whom they could learn about learning and who would support them, most people on campus contribute less effectively to the development of students' understanding than they might. It is only by acting cooperatively in the context of common goals, as the most innovative institutions have done, that our accumulated understanding about learning is put to best use. (American Association for Higher Education, American College Personnel Association, and National Association of Student Personnel Administrators, 1998, p. 1)

Fulfilling the role of educator may require moving beyond a professional comfort zone. Many of us in student affairs have not had the opportunity, either in our graduate preparation programs or in our professional practice, to learn about teaching and learning. Exploring new content, developing new skills, and adapting to new roles all are likely to give rise to cognitive dissonance. This will be particularly true for those who boldly and bravely seek to include critical theoretical perspectives on teaching and learning in their professional practice. Remember the advice we offer students who are afforded similar learning opportunities, and remember the words of Sanford (as adapted by colleagues at IPFW): challenge, support, and celebrate.

Reflective Questions

1. What are your thoughts on the central proposition in this chapter that teaching and learning is, or ought to be, at the center of student affairs professional practice?

2. How has your personal journey to this point helped prepare you to position your professional practice as teaching and learning? Who or what would you identify as principal influences in this regard?

3. This chapter begs an important question. What is the role of education? What are your thoughts on this question?

4. Reflect on a particularly challenging event or issue you have confronted in your professional practice. How might your approach to that event or issue be changed if you construct it through the lens of looking at a teachable moment?

5. Can you identify an instance when you attempted to utilize an educational framework to bring about a change on your campus? How was that effort received? What was the result of the effort? If you are unable to identify such an instance, why is that the case?

7

Reframing Our Professional Practice as Institutional Leaders, Entrepreneurs, and Change Agents

In the late nineteenth century, when Alice Freeman Palmer and LeBaron Russell Briggs assumed their positions at Chicago and Harvard as the first student deans, they had no job description, no professional association, no staff to assist them, no graduate degree in student affairs, and at best, only a vague notion of what was expected of them (Brown, 1928; Palmer, 1908) They literally created their own practice, mainly by watching and listening carefully to their students. But colleges and universities were changing rapidly at that time, resulting in a distancing of many faculty from undergraduates, and so there were many gaps for these new deans to fill and duties to assume that had been overlooked for many years. Deans Palmer and Briggs were both dedicated and visionary educators, and the examples they set caused other institutions to follow the lead of Chicago and Harvard. By 1916, the National Association of Deans of Women was established (Martínez Alemán, 2002), and Lois Kimball Mathews published *The Dean of Women*, the first book dedicated to advancing the young field (Mathews, 1915). In 1919, the men followed with the establishment of the Conference of Deans and Advisers of Men, later to become NADAM in 1929 (Secretarial Notes, 1929).

With these humble beginnings, subsequent student affairs leaders worked diligently to gain acceptance within the academic
community by improving their professional practice, establishing
graduate professional preparation programs (for example, Walter
Dill Scott and Esther Lloyd Jones at Northwestern University),
encouraging the study of psychology and sociology to understand
student behavior, and by demonstrating their competence in the
handling of difficult problems on their campuses.

The history of student affairs is well known to most of those who
practice in the field today and does not need a detailed recounting in
this volume. The student affairs profession is still evolving. There
continues to be a lively debate about what the primary thrust of the
field should be or what should constitute the core of professional
practice. Attempts to impose an orthodoxy of thinking or practice
within the field have rarely succeeded and with 4500 colleges and
universities now serving 20 million students, it is unlikely that
student affairs will be defined in exactly the same manner on every
campus. However, we believe there is general agreement with the
fundamental assumptions and beliefs (National Association of
Student Personnel Administrators, 1989, pp. 11–14) about students
and their learning that drive the work of all student affairs professionals. Even as higher education continues to change, these
fundamental assumptions and beliefs continue to provide the basis
for our professional practice (for a more detailed description, see
Chapter 1).

In this chapter, some of the roles that student affairs leaders have
traditionally assumed will be reviewed, and an argument for reframing our professional practice will be presented, with an emphasis on
student affairs leaders as change agents. Examples will be presented
that illustrate how a reframed professional practice may strengthen
the student affairs role on campus and contribute to enhanced
student growth and learning. We believe becoming effective change
agents is critical to the success of student affairs professionals, to
their institutions, and to the education of their students. The

chapter closes with a summary and some reflective questions for readers to consider in their own professional practice.

Some Roles Student Affairs Leaders Have Assumed

Since student affairs formally began about 120 years ago, leaders have responded to the needs of their institutions, their students, and to major changes in society. Whatever roles they have assumed, they have had to adapt their professional practice to the times. While the various roles described here may seem to be distinct, there is much they have in common, and the best student affairs leaders have been able to move from one to another, depending on what was expected of them.

Adviser, Liaison, Advocate

The earliest deans, without job descriptions or precedent, made their way mainly by watching and listening to students. They knew that any credibility they might earn was dependent upon being accepted and trusted by their students. They were selected by their presidents because they were well known and respected by students and faculty, or because it was felt that their personalities were well suited for the position. The best of them came to know their students well, and in many cases, the parents of their students. As advisers to students on academic, personal, and financial issues, they often influenced the lives of many of them. They also assumed the role of a bridge between students and the institution as faculty became more distant from the personal lives of the students, and at the same time, enabled their presidents to spend more time on broad institutional issues. When they became aware of problems their students faced on campus, whether in student life or in the class-room, they frequently became advocates for openness and fair play. The early deans of women, in particular, faced the most daunting challenges in this regard, as women students were not always welcome on campus and faced exclusion from certain academic majors and student leadership opportunities. Moreover, there were few women as regular faculty members as colleagues or mentors, which added to the difficulties the early women deans encountered.

Counselor, Assessor, Conduct Officer

Especially after World War I, colleges emphasized diagnosis and assessment of students with the aim of advising them to pursue academic programs and careers best suited to their abilities. Strongly influenced by the growing interest in psychology, student affairs leaders viewed their role largely as counselors and advisers, helping students adjust to the demands of college life. Student affairs leaders also assumed the primary judicial role on the campus, formulating and implementing standards of student conduct. During the Great Depression, many student affairs deans helped students with financial and housing concerns, but their role in institution-wide academic and fiscal affairs was tangential. Most student affairs leaders still came from the ranks of the faculty, and few had received formal training for the field in the small number of graduate programs available. But student affairs leaders themselves helped the field advance significantly with the publication of *The Student Personnel Point of View* in 1937 (National Association of Student Personnel Administrators, 1989a). Chapter 1 includes a more detailed discussion of this publication and its impact.

Service Provider, Coordinator of Programs

When enrollments exploded after World War II, colleges were faced with numbers of students they could never have imagined just a few years earlier. Equally important were the returning veterans and the academic, social, and financial needs they introduced to the campuses. Many of the successful adjustments these returning veterans made at colleges and universities were often the result of initiatives taken by student affairs professionals—in such areas as housing, financial aid, recreation, transportation, health services, child care, and academic advising. These services developed rapidly as enrollments continued to soar, and many student affairs leaders assumed the role as coordinator of these services, leading several years later to the position of vice president for student affairs. It was not unusual during this time for enrollments to double and even triple within a period of five years, and in this often chaotic growth period, student affairs professionals helped bring some sense of order to the campus by coordinating these services and making them serve students effectively. Student affairs leaders achieved greater visibility and authority within their area of responsibility on campus, and often were included in meetings with senior administrative officers, but they remained quite separate from the core academic and financial decision-making processes.

Crisis Manager, Institutional Preserver

The professional practice of student affairs was significantly enhanced with the introduction of new ideas and research about how students learn, resulting in the student development movement in the field. Increased attention was paid to individual differences in learning, and in the academic and cocurricular experiences of students that might impact their growth and development. Student affairs professionals viewed their roles as more closely linked with academic programs and student learning, and services such as counseling, career advising, financial aid, and student activities were emphasized.

Two external events—the Civil Rights movement and the Vietnam War—defined this period, and as a result, student affairs professionals were challenged more dramatically than at any time in the history of the field. Because of the successful leadership demonstrated by many student affairs professionals during this time of great unrest, protests, and turmoil on the campuses, the way in which the student affairs role was viewed by students, parents, faculty, presidents, and governing boards was forever changed. Like it or not, many student affairs professionals were evaluated primarily on their ability to deal with volatile issues, demonstrations, and unruly protests. It is ironic that it required this very tumultuous and emotional set of experiences to secure the acceptance and respect for the student affairs field. Some student affairs professionals during this time did not have the skills or the inclination to manage campus crises effectively, and moved on to other professional pursuits. But for those who stayed and survived, the result was a recognition of the value of strong student affairs leaders as essential for the preservation of the campus and an enhanced role in the institution. No one could have predicted that the tumultuous events and issues of the 1960s on campus would have the greatest impact on the growth and success of student affairs. It opened many opportunities to student affairs professionals and greatly influenced how the practice of the field was to be reframed in subsequent years.

New Roles: Institutional Leader, Entrepreneur, and Change Agent

While the new roles of student affairs administrators as institutional leaders, entrepreneurs, and change agents are still emerging, we believe it is clear that this is the direction in which the professional practice is now being reframed. No longer expected to be only crisis managers, forced to become less dependent upon traditional institutional support and buoyed by useful research and insights about student engagement on learning, the best student affairs professionals are now focused on improving their institutions and improving student learning in their role as change agents. They understand the value of teamwork and collaboration with their presidents, administrative peers, and faculty, but at the same time they recognize that if meaningful change is to occur, it will largely be the result of their own skill, determination, and ability to achieve meaningful change. Many of the previous roles assumed by student affairs professionals will continue, but in this reframed professional practice, the emphasis is upon results, self-support, independence, and change. It requires leaders sophisticated about and experienced in organizational theory and change who also have the courage and mettle to take risks in an institutional environment increasingly characterized by intense competition. It also requires leaders who are effective in collaborating with many others and who know that teamwork is essential for success (Love and Estanek, 2004).

The best student affairs professionals have always adapted their actions to the needs of their institutions, the needs and character-istics of their students, the culture of the communities where they are located, the priorities of their presidents, and their own values and beliefs. When major national or international issues have dominated, their own agendas have been determined by forces external to the campus. They have frequently proven their worth to their institutions and their students by their ability and willingness to address issues and needs deemed unpopular or too controversial by others. They have managed to increase mental health services while also providing the primary leadership to crises and incidents of violence on their campuses. They have benefited from a growing research literature within their own field and have made their presence viable within the national higher education community via their professional associations. The new student affairs admin-istrator is emerging as a confident, well-prepared leader who understands the need for change and has the skills and courage to achieve it.

The new student affairs professionals are experts on organiza-tions, but are not wed to only one model or to only one reporting arrangement. They know how to make their voices heard, regardless of the shape of the organizational chart. They understand their role as leaders and know that they will be evaluated mainly by the results they have achieved and the issues they have resolved. While committed to professional development improvements in their own field, they recognize and accept that effective student affairs leaders may come from a variety of academic and experiential backgrounds. They reject the notion that their only function is that of crisis manager or peacekeeper, but willingly continue to assume those leadership roles on their campuses. They are strongly committed to higher education's role in improving opportunity for those still denied access and are determined to support the disadvantaged, the poor, and the unseen. They are passionate advocates for change and for additional institutional financial support, but recognize and accept the reality that if they are going to achieve their goals, they will need to identify and secure most of the resources on their own. But they, like their presidents and academic and administrative colleagues, are also uneasy about the future, uncertain about what forms higher education may assume in the face of dazzling new technological developments and daunting financial constraints.

The uncertainty about the future structure, funding, and form of American higher education presents serious challenges to student affairs professionals as they strive to become change agents on their campuses and to reframe their professional practice. For example, should they work to secure financial support for expensive new facilities, such as residence halls, student centers, and recreation buildings? It is certainly not clear what the eventual impact of MOOCs will be, as technology presents students and institutions with new opportunities for taking courses, anywhere, anytime. Should student affairs professionals concentrate on attracting full-time, residential, traditional age students to their campuses, or should they be actively pursuing online students, regardless of their origin or current location? What investments in student services for online students are needed, and how should these be funded? How should student affairs leaders work with provosts and faculty in improving the undergraduate experience when a substantial proportion of the students are enrolled exclusively in online classes? If the federal student financial aid programs are significantly altered by the Congress, what role should the college assume in this process? Who will assume responsibility for enhancing the existing student affairs graduate preparation programs to ensure that new professional staff will have the skills and knowledge to work effectively with a new student generation who may not be place-bound and is technologically sophisticated? How will diversity, faculty-student relationships, student leadership, and service to others be learned by students whose relationship to their institution is primarily online? These are not hypothetical questions, but ones now actually being faced by student affairs leaders. No one can say with certainty what will happen in the next several years in higher education; however, change is already occurring, and the best student affairs leaders are already engaged in discussions about how they will rethink their professional practice.

Preparing for a Reframed Change Agent Role

As indicated earlier in this chapter, the traditional roles for student affairs professionals—adviser, counselor, advocate, and crisis manager—will continue, but the best leaders will be entrepreneurs and change agents as well. Some student affairs professionals may not feel comfortable in this new role, feeling that such activities as fundraising and initiating change will take them away from their traditional functions. Others may feel they have had no professional preparation to become entrepreneurs or to become actively engaged in the often bruising business of change. We believe that this is an important choice for student affairs professionals to make at a time when higher education is changing rapidly, public support is declining, and increased scrutiny is being given to the actions of institutional leaders. In order to succeed, student affairs professionals need to become more independent, more effective as change agents, and more entrepreneurial in their actions. What can they do to prepare themselves for this role?

As student affairs professionals contemplate what they need to do in order to become more independent and entrepreneurial, they first must decide if this is a role they want to assume and whether they feel confident in doing so. Student affairs professionals have spent their careers as helpers, advisers, counselors, and encouragers, and shifting their priorities can represent a substantive change in how they view themselves and their jobs. However, we believe that this is necessary if student affairs is to continue to be a significant contributor to the success of students and institutions.

Experienced student affairs professionals can learn a great deal by watching and listening—to their colleagues among the faculty, their presidents, their provosts, and their development staff. At research universities, many faculty have become virtually self-supporting for years in a highly competitive environment where their success is dependent upon their own initiatives in obtaining grants to pursue their academic and research goals. Participating with presidents in their efforts to attract more funds, whether through legislative contacts or with potential donors, can prove very valuable to student affairs professionals in learning how to do the same thing in their own areas of interest. Growing numbers of student affairs divisions already have their own development staff, working in cooperation with the overall institutional fundraising program, and student affairs professionals can benefit from the expertise and experience of these experienced fundraisers.

There are many workshops and institutes available to student affairs professionals to learn more about fundraising, their role as change agents, and trends in higher education. Some of these focus on student affairs, but others outside of higher education may also be of benefit. Reading and studying the organizational change literature referred to in Chapter 2 of this book can also help student affairs professionals become more knowledgeable about their new roles.

One of the best ways to learn about how to assume a new role can take place as a result of personal consultation with close colleagues. Those who have already experienced success as more independent, entrepreneurial leaders and change agents on their campuses can be a great resource. There is a tradition within the student affairs field for professionals of openly sharing their learning (both successes and failures!) with one another, and transitioning to a new role presents a good opportunity to do this.

No student affairs professional achieves dramatic success as a change agent or as an entrepreneur overnight. This is a process that requires careful planning and serious study. It is not done alone and will become most effective if done in conjunction with colleagues. The concept of pursuing "small wins" is applicable here. It may take several years and a good deal of patience before significantly more independence is achieved.

Perhaps the most important skill to learn in order to become a successful new change agent–oriented student affairs professional is courage. The willingness to take risks, to place one's ideas and abilities in open competition with others, to have one's proposals scrutinized and criticized, to work effectively with supporters and detractors, and to be able to negotiate to achieve goals are all required. This is not a role for those who are seeking security in their positions; the opportunity to fail is real, but the potential benefits for improved student support and learning are excellent. We believe that the future of student affairs depends on this change-based model for student affairs leaders.

Case Studies

The following brief cases provide illustrations of the strategies used by student affairs professionals in initiating and bringing about change. As with the case studies in the preceding chapters, these are adapted from real-life examples.

A New Retreat Center

The dean of students at a public university had established a very positive tradition of student leadership development, civic engagement, and volunteerism on the campus for many years. She and her staff were well known and respected among students, faculty, and alumni. Through their energetic and creative work with student groups and organizations, they made a very positive contribution to the institution and to its students.

The dean always had a dream of building an off-campus retreat facility that would accommodate about a hundred students for weekend conferences, seminars, and workshops. For about five years, she had her eye on some property located on a lake about ten miles from the campus—an ideal place for students, faculty, and staff to gather for a weekend to learn in a relaxed and open atmosphere. She knew she could not attract state funds for building such a facility, but she loved a challenge and was determined to pursue this dream. She quietly proceeded to devise a strategy to make it a reality.

After visiting a few similar facilities associated with campuses in surrounding states, she shared the concept for the retreat center with an architect friend. Using funds from her own modest discretionary fund, she asked him to accompany her to the site she had in mind and then to sketch a draft of a facility, including meeting rooms, a kitchen, two fireplaces, and sleeping rooms for one hundred people. In just a few weeks, she had in hand three drawings of what such a center might look like and her excitement for the project increased again. She had already contacted a trusted real estate broker in the city to determine if the land she had in mind for the project might be available in the future. After consultation with others, she came to a realistic estimate of the cost of this project—$4 million—and knew that she would have to find ways herself to raise this money.

She knew she would need the approval of her president and vice president for development if she could proceed. With some skepticism, they gave her an initial vote of confidence, so long as any fundraising efforts on her part did not interfere with other, more major projects already under way by the institution. She had created a student affairs advisory board seven years ago, consisting of successful former student leaders, prominent alumni from a variety of backgrounds, and some community leaders as well. This group has been very loyal to the dean and had supported her efforts with students with funds for a variety of functions, including student aid, career planning, and substance abuse education programs. The board was very positive about improving student learning but had never been asked to take on a major project such as this proposed retreat center.

The dean decided to present the proposal to her advisory board. Before she did, she talked in person with each member of the board over a period of a couple of weeks. She also presented the idea to a council of twenty-five top student leaders on the campus and asked several of them to attend the advisory board meeting as well. Her proposal was met with enthusiasm and support by almost everyone, but of course, also by serious concern about how to raise the money.

Over the next five years, the dean, with the assistance of her institutional development staff, convinced various members of her student affairs advisory council to chair five committees composed of alumni and friends of the institution. With strong support from students, this effort proceeded. The dean was also successful in getting her president to actively assist in the fund-raising program.

After five years of hard work, the dean was ready to move ahead with the building of the retreat center (by now, the cost had escalated to $6 million!). She was confident that there was sufficient momentum in the campaign to make it a self-sustaining operation.

Discussion. It required several years to accomplish, and the dean knew she was putting herself and her reputation at stake by trying to do this. But she also understood that if her student affairs division was going to move ahead and become more successful in helping students learn, she needed to assume the leadership in making this happen. The carefully planned actions the dean took, over time, were necessary to move her and others at her institution to her eventual goal. In the process, she used change strategies of having a vision, involving others in decisions, educating herself about what needed to be done, collaborating with others outside the division of student affairs, and developing and gaining the support of an advisory board she recruited to assure the success of this project.

Improving Dining and Food Services

The vice president for student affairs at a small, private, residential college had responsibility for campuswide dining and food services. He had been in his position for three years, having come from a similar college in another state. The food service program on this campus was handled by a private company, with whom the college has had a contract for the past ten years. There was a standing committee that reviews the contract every three years, and it was the decision of the vice president for student affairs whether to renew the contract or amend it in some way.

The vice president was very aware that there was wide dissatisfaction with the quality and efficiency of the food service on campus. Moreover, the private company providing the service had experienced considerable turnover in its leadership during the past few years, and has had difficulty fulfilling its financial obligations to the college. The vice president for student affairs had maintained close contact with company officials, notified them of her dissatisfaction, and told them that if significant improvements were not made within the next six months, it is likely that the contract would be cancelled.

The vice president was an experienced administrator and aware that competition in the food service industry was very strong. He knew there was often a gap between promises and delivery in providing such campus services. Moreover, he was concerned that in the past few years on his campus, the company had placed very little emphasis on healthy foods, opting instead for the more popular nationally branded fast-food outlets with whom it had subcontracted. Finally, the vice president was embarrassed that for special events the president hosted on campus, private, outside caterers were being used in place of the contracted vendor.

The vice president was determined to make real changes in this situation and improve the dining and food services. He knew he needed to discuss the matter again with his food service advisory council, but he also knew he could not rely upon them to suggest very bold actions. He decided to visit three other campuses to observe what they were doing; also, he invited two experienced campus food service leaders to campus to critique the food service situation and to advise him on what he might do. What he had in mind was canceling the current contract with the company and within a period of one year, taking responsibility for operating the campus dining and food service himself.

He was convinced that hiring excellent people to run the campus food service can result in significant improvements in quality, healthy choices, and financial profit. He also knew that doing this was a big risk. If the effort failed, his credibility and effectiveness as vice president would be in serious jeopardy. He had confidence in his ability to make this a success, and he was encouraged when he was able to convince the president and the other key campus administrators to go ahead with the project.

He placed himself on a crash-course of learning everything he could about dining and food services. His campus already had in place most of the essential physical equipment and facilities for a good food service; he knew the most important task he had was hiring a talented staff to give leadership to building and operating the food service program. After involving faculty, students, and staff in the process over a period of several months, the vice president hired a staff who he was convinced shared his goal of providing a healthy, creative, desirable, and profitable food service program.

Three years later, the food service was doing quite well financially and was well accepted on the campus. Of course, the vice president knew that would require constant scrutiny and evaluation. But as far as students, staff, and faculty were concerned, it was no longer an issue.

Discussion. The vice president's strategy was to understand the problem, decide to do something about it, be willing to take a big risk, and collaborate with others. Through hard work and persistence, he was able to bring about needed change. A better food service may not be directly related to the educational goals of the institution, but the vice president was convinced that it was important to the quality of campus life, and it needed to be significantly improved. By taking the initiative as a change agent on this important service, the vice president solidified his role as an important leader on the campus.

Confronting Academic Dishonesty

The dean of students of a medium-size public university had been in her position for four years. She was the senior student affairs officer and reported to the provost. She was also a member of the Council of Deans, which consisted of the leaders of the twelve colleges on the campus and was the most influential and prestigious group on the campus. The university was over 130 years old and enjoyed a solid academic reputation in the Midwest. It had a law school, veterinary school, and several doctoral programs, mainly in the sciences and agriculture. Admission to the undergraduate program was fairly competitive and retention was not a concern. The enrollment had been steadily growing, albeit slowly over the past several years.

The dean of students had earned a reputation as a very personable administrator who was well known on the campus and community for her compassion for students and her commitment to civility. She had not been reluctant to confront issues and policies that she felt her institution should address and, in particular, had become an outspoken advocate for the recruitment and support for economically disadvantaged students.

In her work with students and faculty, the issue of academic dishonesty had frequently been discussed and worried about, but nothing had been done about this in her four years at the university. The dean of students was well read in the extensive literature and research on academic dishonesty and strongly suspected that her campus was no different from most colleges in the substantial percentage of students who admit that they have cheated in their academic coursework. Moreover, she was aware of two studies done by doctoral students on her own campus, both of which confirmed what she suspected: her campus had a serious academic cheating problem.

There were rules about academic honesty in the student hand-book and a procedure for faculty to follow if they find that a student has cheated on an exam or term paper. However, there was no consistency in enforcing this policy among the colleges, and most faculty did not pay much attention to it. There had been discussion in the student government association about an honor code, but nothing had come out of this during the dean's four years at the university. The dean's goal in getting her university to address this issue via the task force on academic integrity was to confront the problem and to do something positive about it.

The dean of students was not naïve and knew that if she decided to confront this issue and tried to improve academic honesty at her campus, she was very likely to face resistance—from her president, from the provost, from academic deans, and from her students. She knew that institutions are often reluctant to admit that they may have such a problem, do not like the negative publicity it may bring, and are frequently skeptical about the survey results that document the problem. Finally, she understood that if she tried to initiate some change in this area, the effort might fail, and she might be viewed as an unrealistic crusader for a lost cause that should be left alone. Nonetheless, she did not want to wait for an ugly cheating scandal to occur on the campus to confront this issue—she knew now would be a good time to start this process, before such a crisis did occur.

After thinking about this matter carefully, she decided to discuss it with the provost. Instead of framing the issue in a negative manner, she presented it as an opportunity to improve academic integrity on the campus. She suggested that if she could gain the support of the Council of Academic Deans, the faculty senate, and the student government association, she would then ask the provost to appoint a task force on academic integrity. The task force would be chaired by a prominent faculty member and would consist of students, faculty, and academic administrators.

After the dean secured the support of the Council of Academic Deans, the faculty senate, and the student government, the provost agreed to appoint a sixteen-member task force to address the issue. The dean of students served as an ex-officio role with the task force and became the primary source of information, policies, and honor codes from other, similar campuses. She also made sure the task force members had frank and credible information about the extent of cheating at their own campus. After thorough study and discussion, the task force made a series of recommendations to the provost and the Council of Academic Deans designed to improve academic integrity at the university. The dean of students was very pleased with this outcome, but knew that she would have to remain very active in the process in the next few years to assure that real improvements will, in fact, take place.

Discussion. The dean of students knew she had no power herself to dictate changes to improve academic integrity at her university, but she knew the issue, knew the obstacles, and knew the culture of her campus in a way that she could make it likely that positive change could take place. Due to the credibility and respect she had built on the campus for many years, and her patience and persistence, she exerted effective leadership as a change agent. Her strategy was to identify the problem realistically, work closely with those whose support was most needed, involve key faculty, administrators, and student leaders in the process, and allow the process sufficient time so that the issue could be considered rationally.

Creating a New Scholarship Program

The academic quality of the undergraduate students at a prestigious private institution was high, and the admissions process was very selective. There was a large endowment in place, which made possible an outstanding and much sought after scholarship for exceptionally gifted students. The fifty students were selected each year for this named scholarship without regard to financial need or geographical location. Having been in place for twenty-five years, the scholarship program earned national prestige for its excellence.

The director of admissions knew that this scholarship program had enhanced the already distinguished reputation of the university and was a matter of considerable pride to the institution. However, the director of admissions also was keenly aware that the overwhelming majority of the recipients of the scholarship were white students from affluent, well-educated families. He believed his institution also had an obligation to provide outstanding educational opportunities to a broader, more diverse, and less privileged segment of the population. He wanted to convince his institution to consider a plan to alter the nature of the student body to become more inclusive and economically diverse.

He knew that the prestigious scholarship program in place was so revered by the governing board, the faculty, and the alumni that it would be almost impossible to change. He also knew that to convince his institution that it should place an equal amount of endowment money into a program specifically targeting first generation students from poor families would take a lot of effort and persuasion. He was convinced that the potential benefits for the students and for his institution were great, but he felt he could not do this by himself.

The director of admissions compiled a succinct report that documented information about the current students, including their socio-economic backgrounds, their racial and ethnic backgrounds, and their families' educational attainments. He then compared these data with national demographics to demonstrate how dramatically nonrepresentative his institution had become. He also obtained student profiles from three equally prestigious private universities, all of which had more diverse students than his institution, especially in terms of family income and ethnic and racial background. He knew this information was necessary but insufficient in itself to convince his institution to create a new scholarship program for talented first generation students from poor families.

He quietly shared information about successful scholarship programs at other selective private colleges with the provost (to whom he reported), the faculty, his president, and, with the president's permission, with the development director. Over a period of about two years, he was able to generate considerable enthusiasm for his idea. He and his provost then invited their counterpart academic leaders from another selective private college who had started a similar program just four years ago to come to the campus and discuss their effort. The president now was convinced that this new program aimed at first generation students from poor families was not only the right thing to do at the institution, but also was something urgently needed. The president and provost knew that such a program would require a substantial permanent endowment, similar to the existing scholarship program. It became their goal to name the new program and fund it in a similar manner as the established program. The director of admissions was delighted and was thrilled that in the next three years, members of the governing board responded with a special fundraising program that successfully raised a $50 million endowment to support it. The director of admissions was placed in charge of this new scholarship program designed to attract academically talented, low-income, first generation students to the institution.

Discussion. The director of admissions was able to convince his institutional leaders to reexamine the values and mission of the university and to consider how they could realize their educational goals through a special scholarship program. He knew the issues, had built his own credibility on the campus for some years, and took his time in cultivating the support of key decision makers. His strategy as a change agent in this process was to rely on his credibility, learn to be persuasive with others, to share useful information from competitor institutions, suggest realistic solutions to the problem, and demonstrate patience. His actions resulted in a very successful outcome for his institution and confirmed his role as an important contributor to improved educational opportunities for students.

Conclusion

Becoming a strong student affairs leader who can make change happen at an institution does not occur overnight. It requires patience, study, and keen insight into the culture and values of an institution. It also requires courage, as leaders place themselves at risk by proposing new ideas and programs and by openly advocating changes that others may find threatening or unnecessary. Successful leaders rarely, if ever, accomplish things by themselves; they learn they must work with many others—on and off campus—to build support for their ideas and proposals. They learn to work with others who may not share their vision and priorities and to adjust their plans in order to fulfill their goals. They learn that almost no one ever accomplishes every single aspect of a plan or program, but that progress usually comes in stages and that improvements can be added over time.

They may have to think hard about whether they are able or willing to assume a more aggressive role as a change agent, and what this may imply for their own role within their institution. They may decide that their own professional background and experience are not well suited to this new role or that they would prefer a less visible or volatile administrative life. The student affairs profession is now diverse and extensive in the various positions and services it provides on campuses, and not every professional is well suited to become a senior leader and change agent. But the need is clear, and the advancement and success of the profession depend on reframing the student affairs professional as an agent of change.

The risks may seem daunting for those student affairs professionals who want to reframe themselves as leaders of change, but the potential rewards for better student learning are worth taking. If this is done, we believe the student affairs profession will be moving in the right direction.

Reflection Questions

1. How can I best learn the skills to become a change-oriented student affairs leader?

2. What implications does this change agent role have for professional and graduate preparation programs?

3. Can effective change take place during difficult budgetary times?

4. In considering a new leadership position at a college or university, how can I assess the openness of the institution to change?

5. What power do student affairs professionals have on their campuses? Can you define the nature of this power?

8

Looking Toward the Future

Examples of successful change efforts driven by dedicated professionals abound in higher education. Less than four decades ago women students were treated in a manner that was substantially different from that for male students on many dimensions, including having curfews or hours imposed on them while male students were free to come and go as they liked. Change has certainly happened for women. Less than three decades ago online registration of students was experimental, and many were concerned that the system would break down and students would never be assigned to classes. Yet by purposeful leadership, with a plan, online registration has become the norm on most campuses. Less than two decades ago few, if any, colleges or universities had developed crises management plans. We have learned, however, that it is necessary and it is now the norm on most campuses.

Changes in society, technology, changes in curriculum, and changes in the demographics of the student body have all brought new challenges and opportunities to higher education. Some of these changes occurred because of events in the greater society, including legal decisions and changed societal attitudes. Some of the changes have occurred because of events within institutions that made change inevitable. For example, a long-serving president retired; a donor made a substantial gift for a new academic program; or a new dean or vice president was appointed. Many of the changes experienced by institutions of higher education, however, occurred because someone questioned why the institution did things in certain ways and brought a new perspective to issues faced by students, faculty, and staff.

We believe an essential role for student affairs professionals is to be an intentional change agent to improve the student experience and the community experience of higher education. If a student affairs professional decides to be a change agent, he or she should consider both what they want to change and *why* they feel a change is needed. Change with the sole purpose to shake things up usually is not successful in the long term. Change that is purposeful, transparent, and clear can make a significant difference in the quality of the educational experiences of students, as well as the experiences of the faculty and staff who work with them.

Transparency requires the change agent to

- Clearly articulate how the proposed change aligns with the values of the institution

- Acknowledge how the proposed change will affect the students, faculty, and staff impacted by the change

- Provide a description of what will *not* happen if the change is not adopted

The role of a change agent is not an easy one, nor is it without controversy, and we understand that some of our colleagues will not feel comfortable in that role. However, we believe that encouraging fresh perspectives on old issues and intentionally becoming an agent of change within our institutions is essential for success in the future. Case studies were used throughout the volume to illustrate the many ways that student affairs professionals can be change agents on their campus. Important changes can occur with a specific student or staff member, within a student organization, within a department, within the division of student affairs, or within the institution. The cases used throughout the volume illustrated how to apply what we know to improve the educational and personal growth experience for students.

Strategies That Enhance the Success of Change in Higher Education

Whether we are discussing effective and meaningful use of resources, applying theory, research, and data to gain understanding of problems, using technology effectively, actively using our foundational and ethical documents, or being intentional about what we are teaching to students, some common perspectives to leading change can be found in the chapters and case studies in this volume. We have identified twelve themes that are important to remember if you want to be a change agent in your professional role.

Be Intentional

Change can happen by accident, but long-lasting, positive change needs to be intentional and goal directed. Just saying that something has to change is not enough. First, if possible find out why the specific program, process, or procedure was initiated. Understanding what preceded the current state of affairs provides important information for your approach to change. Second, develop a plan to guide the steps to achieving change. As you think about a change seek advice from colleagues both in your own institution and beyond. What pitfalls could occur and what rewards might happen usually can be identified by others who have had experience with the particular change you are interested in implementing. Good ideas often become great ideas because the originator sought out and listened to other perspectives.

Be an active educator as you plan change. Teach and learn at the same time, for if you are modeling being an active learner you are teaching those you come in contact with how to become active learners themselves. Set short-range, mid-range, and long-range goals for the change you wish to make and articulate those to others.

Be Willing to Adapt and Adopt

While a plan is essential, it should not be written in stone. As new information and new data become available, adapt the plan to account for new perspectives but remember to keep your eye on the goal. Be open to ideas that come from outside your own experiences and listen carefully to the perspectives of others. While the use of theory, for example, can provide a valuable lens to examine a problem, be willing to adapt your plan to accommodate the unique differences of institutional structures and the larger context. The strategies you use might be altered depending on what you learn from reading the literature and research or discussing your ideas with others. Always focus on the goal to improve the educational experience of students as you implement change.

Understand the Institution and Its Culture

Each college and university is different. As you develop your plans for change, invest time in understanding the culture and values of the institution and test to see that your idea is congruent with both. Colleagues are invaluable sources of both information and perspective and often can explain why a policy or a program came into being. Understanding what has happened before and why a specific policy or program was created is invaluable when contemplating a change in that policy or program. Is that need being met through other means now? If so, how? Why do you think a change is needed? Being clear, concise, and direct helps others understand the direction and the meaning of the change you wish to institute. What other changes are occurring within the institution? Is the time right for this particular change or do you need to wait a while before introducing your idea?

Seek Partners and Build Partnerships

Rarely does meaningful change occur if one person alone tries to implement a change. No matter how large or how small the issue involved, working with others and creating partnerships to develop solutions is an essential element of achieving successful sustainable change. As you seek partners in the change process be sure you define for yourself what the most important issues are that you are seeking to change, as well as the intended and unintended conse-quences of adapting the plan to include the agendas of others. A common agenda must be defined before a partnership can be formed and a plan for change implemented. Partners bring support and new ideas and approaches, and they can usually help identify pitfalls that might cause the change agenda to fail. So be open to partnerships—you can learn a lot and gain a lot of support.

How You Approach Change Is as Important as Why You Are Seeking Change

How decisions are made is just as important as the decisions that are made. If change is forced, coerced, or imposed it depends too much on who is making the change rather than why the change has been made. If we have been successful in integrating the ethical principles we believe in into the decision-making process, it is likely not to be seen as a power move but rather a jointly conceived idea for improvement. Being open to input, listening respectfully to others, and slowing the process down can sometimes create a great positive difference in how change is perceived. Change that happens in a purposeful and planned way is easier to understand and is less anxiety-producing for all members of the campus community. Transparency is a key element in developing a successful change strategy.

Be Patient with the Process

If you are a dedicated to change, do not try to accomplish everything in one big step. Small wins are important, and as long as they contribute to the goal you want to accomplish then enjoy a small win. But do not stop with small wins and keep your eye on the goal. Prepare for the next step and implement it. Sometimes back planning is a good way to conceptualize change. For example, if you want to change the process of how seniors sign up for job interviews in the Career Center, what will need to happen the day before the new process takes place, the week before, the month before, and so forth. Such an exercise brings structure to the amorphous nature of the change process.

Involve the People Who Will Be Affected by the Change

Often students, faculty, and staff feel that change is something that is being done "to" them rather than "with" them. Even if it brings consternation or concerns to the surface that must be dealt with, involving those who will be affected by the change in the planning and implementation of the change process will make a huge difference in its success. In addition, it is also an effective way to bring new active partners into the implementation process. One word of caution is needed. Students often view the time frame when change needs to happen in relationship to their own enrollment and the eventual award of their degree. Honesty on the time frame to affect a specific change is a key element in working with students on new ideas.

Stay Current

Take the time to stay current with professional literature and research. Identify what is of interest to you and figure out why it intrigues you. Staying current with new ideas, new research, and new methods helps us keep our minds open to change opportunities within our own environment. We understand that staying current takes time, but the investment is well worth the effort. Some student affairs professionals have initiated informal lunch groups where each member takes responsibility for reading one journal each month and provides highlights and references for the use of others in the group. It is one way to keep up to date, and the fact that you regularly meet together may present new opportunities for implementing needed changes.

In addition, participate in conferences and workshops to learn about cutting-edge ideas and programs. Being an active learner is an essential characteristic of an effective change agent. Finally, contribute to the literature and share your ideas with others for feedback and inspiration.

Look Within and Without

Look both within the student affairs literature and without the field for new ideas, new theories, and new approaches. By not confining our learning to what is familiar we are much more likely to learn something new. Take advantage of the learning opportunities available within your academic community. Attend lectures, plays, and concerts even if at first glance you think it is not something that you are particularly interested in. Student affairs professionals work in an environment that is focused on learning, and your own openness to learning can be a powerful tool when trying to influence change.

Manage Resources Effectively

If you cannot effectively manage the human, physical, and fiscal resources assigned to your area then you are not likely to become an agent of change. Solid performance on routine matters brings credibility to a change agent. In addition, if new resources are needed to implement the needed change then you are more likely to receive such support if you have a track record as a good resource manager. Often a new program or a policy change can be seen as having greater risk than remaining with what is already in place. It is unlikely, for example, that computer mediated instruction would have been implemented on many campuses if the underlying technical structure for it had not been effectively managed. Being a good steward of the resources for which you are responsible increases your credibility as a change agent. For more information and ideas about effective resource management see Chapter 3 in this volume.

Remember the Whole Student

When you are proposing change, identify how it will affect the whole student. Take a step back from any proposal to determine if it really will have a positive influence in the lives of students or if it is a change that just makes life easier for faculty and staff. Some changes are needed but the processes involved are invisible to students. The result of the change should, however, result in improved waiting times, less red tape, or some other impact that will improve the experience of students. For example, a change in requirements can affect the financial plan and support for students, so how can that be accounted for in the planned change? Or think about the ease of access for students with physical disabilities when changing the venue for a program and plan for accommodations. Our foundational documents still provide excellent guidance to us as we plan for the future. Examining the possible impact of a change on students and involving them in planning for the change can reduce many of these concerns.

Have Courage and Take Risks

Becoming a change agent is not for the timid or fearful; often it is much easier to just accept what is rather than examining new approaches and solutions. But "we have always done it this way" is a mantra on many campuses, but overcoming the resistance to change is one of the largest hurdles a change agent can face. Why do we do it this way? What may be a better way? Who will be affected by any change? What will be lost if a change is adopted? All these are legitimate but difficult questions for a campus community.

One of the most important roles of a change agent is to speak up for those whose voices are lost or overlooked on the campus. Helping them find a voice can be risky in some institutions, but someone needs to advocate for those members of the community. Often such actions are not seen as positive and there is resistance within the community. But have courage and do what you think is right. In the long run, the campus community will be better for it!

What Will the Future Bring?

Change will continue to happen in higher education. As we contemplate the future we believe the following questions will provide both the greatest challenges and the greatest opportunities for the student affairs profession. Each has challenges and opportunities for student affairs professionals to be positive leaders for change as we face the future. Start thinking about them, for some of these changes are already happening and if we are not prepared to act we will be doing a disservice to our students and our institutions. It may be useful to use these questions to guide staff discussions about the future for students and student affairs on your specific campus. Identifying issues when they are small can often avoid a crises situation in the future.

- **As student bodies become more diverse, how can student affairs help create supportive and inclusive learning communities on their campuses?**

Our student bodies change every year and become more diverse in terms of ethnicity, race, religion, family circumstances, economic background, age, and other dimensions. As those changes often are gradual it is important to stop and examine the data each year to see the amount of change within the student body. Are more students part-time and if so what are the implications for student affairs? Are more students from challenged financial circumstances? Are more students older with family responsibilities? And what is the institution's response to their unique needs? Do you have more students enrolled with both seen and unseen disabilities? Are more students enrolled from a specific racial or ethnic background, and if so do they have unmet needs? Has religious diversity come to your campus, and how is that diversity manifesting itself in the life of the campus?

What does the literature and research tell you about what methods work to create active and supportive learning communities with diverse students? What do the students currently enrolled need and want? How can your institution best respond? These are not easy questions but they will become more prevalent, and reflective student affairs programs will adjust programs and services to meet the needs of an ever changing student body. Each institution and student affairs organization will need to develop their own responses to a changed student body. A great challenge but a rewarding one as students flourish in a community of learning.

- **What potential roles can student affairs play in the growing arena of online education?**

Already many of our students are enrolling in online courses while enrolled in traditional classes. Online education is not just for students in distant locations but is also utilized by many traditional and non-traditional students enrolled full-time at an institution. Those students have access to many of the traditional services and programs provided by student affairs, including psychological care, career counseling and placement, programming, and the like.

The more vexing questions include what should the role of student affairs be for students who are distance learners, and how can we assist faculty who are concerned about students enrolled in their online classes? Is there a way to bring some services to students online without compromising quality? What outreach programs can be developed for faculty teaching online classes? What can the institution do about a student who is exhibiting disturbed and disturbing behavior to an online instructor? Should online students pay the same fees as students enrolled on campus if they cannot directly access services? These questions and others need to be answered to help define the role of student affairs in online education. These discussions should already be under way on most campuses, and if they are not, student affairs professionals should begin the discussion.

- **With concern being raised by many sources regarding the affordability and cost of higher education, what can reasonably be done to reduce escalating costs?**

In many states an easy answer is being put forth by state legislatures and others. The question is seen as one of economics, and the easy answer is to pay concerted attention to degree completion within a four-year period at senior colleges and universities instead of taking five or six years to acquire an undergraduate degree. However, for some students life circumstances intervene, including family responsibilities, financial issues, and personal issues. So while supporting degree completion in four years is appropriate for some students this is not a case where one solution fits all students.

Another part of the answer relates to streamlining the articulation process between community colleges and senior colleges and universities. This may include focusing more on what courses will transfer for full credit and developing some joint advising processes between community and senior colleges. More work needs to be done on these issues.

In addition, some institutions have developed new tuition pricing structures for students entering and remaining at their institution. Other institutions are reducing their general budget allocations to intercollegiate athletics and increasing efforts in fundraising in order to be less dependent on state funding. Whatever the answer, clarity and transparency will be necessary as institutions deal with the cost of higher education.

- **With specialization becoming more prevalent in student affairs organizations, what is needed to create a common understanding of the foundations, assumptions, beliefs, ethics, and theoretical constructs of student affairs?**

Student affairs organizations have grown over the years, and many new functions have come under the student affairs umbrella. For example, campus recreation, health services, food services, services for students with disabilities, and expanded psychological services bring new professionals with diverse backgrounds to the student affairs staff. Assumptions should not be made about the understandings these new to student affairs professionals have. Staff orientation programs within the division of student affairs are usually useful in helping everyone work from a common understanding of the goals and purposes of student affairs. Developing a curriculum for new staff orientation can focus those efforts on common understandings and purposes of serving students and/or institutions.

Discussions throughout the year expose staff new to the division to our foundational documents, and ethical statements help build a common understanding about the beliefs that undergird our work. Finally, this integration is something that should involve the senior student affairs officers in order to underscore the commitment to these assumptions and beliefs. In tight economic times devoting time to staff development can be seen as frivolous when there are students to be served. Making common understandings a basic expectation of all members of the staff, however, is too important to be left to chance. Investment of time and modest resources will result in a more cohesive staff better attuned to working with the whole student.

- **What should the role of student affairs be when dealing with dual enrollment students (those taking college credit courses in their high schools or on campus)?**

The number of students taking college credit courses while enrolled in high school is growing across the country. The growth of this group of students raises new questions for student affairs professionals. First, what role (if any) should campus-based student affairs units have in serving these students? Second, assuming there is some role, how should student affairs programs and services be shaped in order to support the success of these students? Questions include the following:

What should be the content of orientation programs for dual enrollees?

What are the developmental issues facing these students?

What growth opportunities are they missing by not having a traditional freshman year experience?

How should records be handled by the institution or the high school?

How are academic dishonesty questions resolved for such students in college courses? By the high school or the higher education institution? What standards should apply?

Should the privacy standards of the high schools or the collegiate institutions prevail?

Obviously there are many questions that need to be addressed. Student affairs should assume leadership in bringing these and other issues to the table for debate and resolution.

- **As state laws change with regard to legalization of the use of marijuana, what are the potential implications for student affairs and institutions of higher education?**

As laws change and the use of certain drugs is decriminalized there are real implications for student affairs staff and the institutions and students they serve. Just because something is legal should it be allowed in an educational setting? Are there different limitations that can be set for buildings and for general institutional grounds? Can a legal substance be banned from a public campus or a private one? Should legalized drugs be banned? These questions need to be faced and answered prior to the time that legalization of currently banned substances occurs. The questions are vexing and not easily answered but student affairs should provide leadership to the discussion and the implications of any decisions that are made.

- **How can technological advances help or hinder the work of student affairs?**

Changes in technology, including social media, seem to happen on a daily basis. Keeping up with changes and deciding what is appropriate and what is not can be a daunting task for the uninitiated and uninformed. How many resources should be devoted to implementing new technology and new ways of interacting with students on social media? Who is going to be responsible for assuring updates and accuracy of the online presence of student affairs at any institution? These questions and many others associated with technology will need to be answered in the future in a thoughtful way that focuses on the effectiveness of communication and interaction with students through technology.

- **As fiscal resources for higher education have diminished there has been increased pressure for student affairs to fund programs on a fee-for-service basis. What implications does this have for student affairs and the students we serve?**

A-fee-for services model is not new to higher education, but there are both obvious and hidden implications for adopting this model in some units. For example, often those most in need of the services may not be able to afford additional fees. How does this affect students with long-term mental health issues, physical disabilities, or diseases that need expensive medications? It is unclear how the new Affordable Care Act will influence the discussion of moving student affairs agencies to a fee-for-services basis, but it is an issue the needs to be faced sooner rather than later.

- **How will the new legislation at the national and state level affect student health insurance programs, particularly for international students?**

Many institutions require students to have health insurance through another program or through the institution's own health insurance plan. What are the implications for student insurance programs and students older than twenty-five who may not be covered by insurance plans through their families? Can health insurance be made available to them at reasonable prices, and if it can't what alternatives are available for health care? As more colleges embrace internationalization activities this question will become even more pressing.

- **How can more men be attracted to the field of student affairs?**

After many years of being concerned about opportunities for women in higher education, student affairs has a new question to answer. The data are clear—each year more women than men enter the field, more men than women leave the field, and the lack of balance is already beginning to be of concern to thoughtful professionals in the field. What can be done to attract and retain men in the field of student affairs, and should anything be intentionally done?

- **What should be the role of student affairs in study abroad programs?**

The majority of study abroad students are traditionally aged undergraduates. As they study abroad they are living in cultures with laws and expectations sometimes radically different from their experiences at home. Student affairs should be actively involved during the orientation to the study abroad experience. In addition, student affairs should assist in planning for personal and psychological emergencies that might be experienced by students studying abroad. Assuring that notification procedures are in place and consultation is available to students and the staff that are working with them when difficult circumstances arise is an essential function for student affairs. Finally, when students return from their experience student affairs should welcome them home and aid in their reintegration into the campus community.

- **What changes are needed in graduate preparation programs for student affairs?**

Preparation programs certainly cannot do everything, but considerations should be given to helping students translate what they have learned into everyday decisions in their professional lives. It is only through such intentional efforts that students will be able to integrate the knowledge they learned in graduate preparation programs into their professional practice. Active use of case studies, guided internships, and encouragement of students to write about what they have learned can reinforce their learning and help them be better prepared to help students in the future.

Conclusion

These questions are among the most pressing issues facing higher education and student affairs. We raise them with the hope that they will stimulate discussion about the future of student affairs and higher education. Dealing with change is not an easy task, but student affairs professionals should assume a strong leadership role in assuring that our institutions are supportive learning environments for all students. We are confident that the student affairs profession has the talent, the knowledge, and the skills to continue to make a significant contribution to the education of all students.

References

Allen, C., Edmonds, C., Parker, B., and Bach, J. Using LGBTQ Young Adult Literature with University Student Affairs Professionals. *SIGNAL Journal*, Fall/Winter, 2012.

American Association for Higher Education, American College Personnel Association, and National Association of Student Personnel Administrators. *Powerful Partnerships: A Shared Responsibility for Learning*. Washington, D.C., 1998. Accessed on January 30, 2014 at http://www.acpa.nche.edu/sites/default/files/taskforce_powerful_partnerships_a_shared_responsibility_for_learning.pdf.

American Association of State Colleges and Universities. *Creating a New Compact Between States and Public Higher Education*. Washington, D.C.: Author, 2013.

American College Personnel Association. *The Student Learning Imperative: Implications for Student Affairs*. Washington, D.C.: Author, 1996. Accessed on August 20, 2013 at http://www.myacpa.org/sli/sli.htm.

American College Personnel Association. *Statement of Ethical Principles and Standards*. Washington, D.C.: Author, 2006. Accessed on January 22, 2014 at http://faculty.uca.edu/kevinh/ACPAEthicsStatement.pdf.

American College Personnel Association, and the National Association of Student Personnel Administrators. *Principles of Good Practice for Student Affairs*. Washington, D.C.: Authors, 1997. Accessed on September 2, 2013 at http://www.acpa.nche.edu/pgp/principle.htm.

American College Personnel Association, and National Association of Student Personnel Administrators. *ACPA and NASPA Professional Competency Areas for Student Affairs Practitioners*. Washington, D.C.: Authors, 2010a. Accessed on August 20, 2013 at http://www.naspa.org/regions/regioniii/Professional Competency.pdf.

American College Personnel Association, and National Association of Student Personnel Administrators. *Envisioning the Future of Student Affairs.* Washington, D.C.: Authors, 2010b. Accessed on March 17, 2013 at http://www.naspa.org/consolidation/TF_final_narr.pdf.

American Council on Education. The Student Personnel Point of View. *American Council on Education Studies,* 6(13), 1949. Accessed on January 22, 2014 at http://www.myacpa.org/sites/default/files/student-personnel-point-of-view-1949.pdf.

Argyris, C. *On Organizational Learning* (2nd ed.). Oxford: Blackwell Publishing, 1999.

Argyris, C., and Schön, D. *Theory in Practice: Increasing Professional Effectiveness.* San Francisco: Jossey-Bass, 1974.

Arum, R., and Roksa, J. *Academically Adrift: Limited Learning on College Campuses.* Chicago: University of Chicago Press, 2011.

Association of Governing Boards of Universities and Colleges. Mission, MOOCs, and Money. *Trusteeship,* 1(21), 2013. Accessed on August 4, 2013 at http://agb.org/trusteeship/2013/1/mission-moocs-money.

Atherton, J. S. *Learning and Teaching; Cognitive Dissonance and Learning.* Learningandteaching.info. Accessed on September 3, 2013 at http://www.learningandteaching.info/learning/dissonance.htm.

Aviles, K., Phillips, B., Rosenblatt, T., and Vargas, J. If Higher Education Listened to Me . . . *EDUCAUSE Review* 40(5), 2005.

Bandura, A. *Social Learning Theory.* Englewood Cliffs, NJ: Prentice Hall, 1977.

Banta, T. W. *Building a Scholarship of Assessment.* San Francisco: Jossey-Bass, 2002.

Baxter Magolda, M. B. Three Elements of Self-Authorship. *Journal of College Student Development,* 49(4), 2008. Accessed on August 20, 2013 at http://www.changemag.org/Archives/Back Issues/2012/January-February 2012/learning-partnerships-full.html.

Baxter Magolda, M. B. Building Learning Partnerships. *Change,* January/February, 2012.

Baxter Magolda, M. B., and Magolda, P. M. What Counts as "Essential" Knowledge for Student Affairs Educators? In P. M. Magolda and M. B. Baxter Magolda (Eds.), *Contested Issues in Student Affairs: Diverse Perspectives and Respectful Dialogue.* Sterling, VA: Stylus Publishing, 2011.

Bean, J. P., and Metzner, B. S. A Conceptual Model of Nontraditional Undergraduate Student Attrition. *Review of Educational Research* 55(4), 1985.

Beloit College. *Mindset List.* Beloit, WI: Author, 2013. Accessed on September 2, 2013 at http://www.beloit.edu/mindset/.

Biddix, J., and Schwartz, R. Walter Dill Scott and the Student Personnel Movement. *NASPA Journal*, 49(3), 2012.

Blake, J. H. The Crucial Role of Student Affairs Professionals in the Learning Process. In E. L. Moore (Ed.), *Student Affairs Staff as Teachers*. New Directions for Student Services, #117, 2007.

Blimling, G., and Whitt, E. *Principles of Good Practice for Student Affairs*. Washington D.C.: American College Personnel Association and National Association of Student Personnel Administrators, 1997. Accessed on August 20, 2013 at http://www.acpa.nche.edu/pgp/principle.htm.

Bolman, L. G., and Deal, T. E. *Reframing Organizations: Artistry, Choice, and Leadership* (2nd ed.). San Francisco: Jossey-Bass, 1997.

Bowen, W. G. *Higher Education in the Digital Age*. Princeton, NJ: Princeton University Press, 2013.

Boyer, E. *Scholarship Reconsidered: Priorities of the Professoriate*. Washington, D.C.: Carnegie Foundation for the Advancement of Teaching, 1990.

Brookfield, S. D. *The Power of Critical Theory: Liberating Adult Learning and Teaching*. San Francisco: Jossey-Bass, 2005.

Brown, R. W. *Dean Briggs*. New York: Harper and Brothers, 1926.

Bureau, D. A. *"Making Them My Own": Student Affairs Master's Students Socialization to Professional Values*. Tucson, AZ: University of Arizona, 2011. Accessed on August 15, 2013 at https://scholarworks.iu.edu/dspace/bitstream/handle/2022/13713/Bureau_indiana_0093A_11084.pdf?sequence=1.

Burke, W. W. *Organization Change: Theory and Practice* (2nd ed.). Thousand Oaks, CA: Sage, 2007.

Cabellon, E. *The Student Affairs Technology Unconferences*. Posted July 25, 2013a. Accessed on August 4, 2013 at http://edcabellon.com/tech/satechun/.

Cabellon, E. *Your Student Affairs 'Selfie.'* EduUniverse. 2013b. Accessed on August 7, 2013 at http://eduniverse.org/your-student-affairs-'selfie'.

Carnegie Foundation for the Advancement of Teaching. *Carnegie Academy for the Scholarship of Teaching and Learning*. Washington, D.C.: Author, 2013. Accessed on August 31, 2013 at http://www.carnegiefoundation.org/scholarship-teaching-learning.

Carpenter, S., and Stimpson, M. T. Professionalism, Scholarly Practice, and Professional Development in Student Affairs. *NASPA Journal*, 44(2), 2007.

Chritton, S. *Personal Branding for Dummies*. Hoboken, NJ: For Dummies, 2012.

Chronicle of Higher Education. *Chronicle of Higher Education Almanac, 2012*. Chronicle of Higher Education, 59(38), 2012.

Cole-Avent, G. A. *An Information Technology Perspective on the Knowledge Skills and Support Services That Lead to Technological Fluency Among College Student Affairs Professionals*. Ann Arbor, MI: University of Michigan, 2008. Accessed on August 4, 2013 at http://purl.galileo.usg.edu/uga_etd/cole-avent_gail_a_200805_phd.

Council for the Advancement of Standards. *CAS Statement of Shared Ethical Principles*. Washington, D.C.: Council for the Advancement of Standards, 2006.

Creswell, J. W. *Research Design: Qualitative, Quantitative, and Mixed Methods Approaches* (4th ed.). Thousand Oaks, CA: SAGE Publications, 2013.

Dalton, J., Crosby, P. C., Valente, A., and Eberhardt, D. Maintaining and Modeling Everyday Ethics in Student Affairs. In G. S. McClellan, and J. Stringer (Eds.), *The Handbook of Student Affairs Administration* (3rd ed.). San Francisco: Jossey-Bass, 2009.

Davis, J. E. *The American Male Imperative: Implications for Addressing Retention and Academic Success*. Washington, D.C.: Association of Public and Land-Grant Universities, 2013.

Desler, M. K. Translating Theory and Assessment Results to Practice. In M. J. Barr, and M. K. Desler (Eds.), *The Handbook of Student Affairs Administration* (2nd ed.). San Francisco: Jossey-Bass, 2000.

DiMaggio, P. J., and Powell, W. The Iron Cage Revisited: Institutional Isomorphism and Collective Rationality in Organizational Fields. *American Sociological Review*, 48, 147–160, 1983.

Doyle, A. *Tips for Building Your Professional Brand*. About.com, 2013. Accessed on August 7, 2013 at http://jobsearch.about.com/od/professionalbranding/qt/brandbuilding.htm.

Drake, M. *Rural Students and Challenges with Technology*. Evolllution.com, 2013. Accessed on August 30, 2013 at http://www.evolllution.com/accessibility/rural-students-and-challenges-with-technology/.

Duderstadt, J. J. *Higher Education in the Digital Age: Technology Issues and Strategies for American Colleges and Universities*. Westport, CT: Praeger Publishing, 2002.

Dungy, G. J. Pedagogies Outside the Classroom. *On Campus with Women*, 34(1–2), 2004. Accessed at http://www.aacu.org/ocww/volume34_1/national.cfm?section=1 on March 24, 2014.

Erwin, T. D. *Assessing Student Learning and Development: A Guide to the Principles, Goals, and Methods of Determining College Outcomes*. San Francisco: Jossey-Bass, 1991.

Evans, N. J., and Guido, F. M. Response to Patrick Love's "Informal Theory": A Rejoinder. *Journal of College Student Development, 53*(2), 2012.

Evans, N. J., Forney, D. S., Guido, F. M., Patton, L. D., and Renn, K. A. *Student Development in College: Theory, Research, and Practice* (2nd ed.). San Francisco: Jossey-Bass, 2010.

Fox, M., Lowe, S., and McClellan, G. S. (Eds.). *Serving Native American Students.* New Directions for Student Services, #109. San Francisco: Jossey-Bass, 2005.

Freire, P. *Pedagogy of the Oppressed.* New York: Continuum, 1970.

Freire, P. *Pedagogy of Hope.* New York: Continuum, 1994.

Fried, J. (Ed.). *Shifting Paradigms in Student Affairs: Culture, Context, Teaching and Learning.* Washington, D.C.: American College Personnel Association, 1995.

Fulmer, R. M., and Keys, J. B. A Conversation with Peter Senge: New Developments in Organizational Learning. *Organizational Dynamics, 27*(2), pp. 33–42, 1998.

Gemmill, E., and Peterson, M. Technology Use Among College Students: Implications for Student Affairs Professionals. *NASPA Journal, 43*(2), 2006: 280–300.

Giroux, H. A. *Border Crossings: Cultural Workers and the Politics of Education.* New York: Routledge, 1992.

Glassick, C. E., Huber, M. T., and Maeroff, G. I. *Scholarship Assessed: Evaluation of the Professoriate.* San Francisco: Jossey-Bass, 1997.

Graham, J. *The Technological Boom: Helpful or Overwhelming?* Keuka Park, NY: Keuka College, 2011. Accessed on August 4, 2013 at http://life.keuka.edu/ 2011/04/15/the-technological-boom-helpful-or-overwhelming/.

Greenleaf, R. K. *Servant Leadership: A Journey into the Nature of Legitimate Power and Greatness* (25th anniversary edition). Mahwah, NJ: Paulist Press, 2012.

Grieve, K., Hopkins, H., McClellan, G., Sachs, M., and Wong, J. *Students on Community: What Is It, Does It Matter, and Are We In?* Presented at the NASPA National Conference in Philadelphia, PA, March 2011.

Guidry, K. R. *When Did Student Affairs Begin Discussing Technology as Competency.* Author, 2012a. Accessed on July 13, 2013 at http://mistakengoal.com/blog/ 2012/04/03/when-did-student-affairs-begin-discussing-technology-as-a-competency/.

Guidry, K. R. *Ongoing Research into Student Affairs Technology History.* Author, 2012b. Accessed on July 13, 2013 at http://mistakengoal.com/blog/2012/06/ 22/ongoing-research-into-student-affairs-technology-history/.

Gupta, U. G. Technophobia Is Conquerable. *StudentAffairsOnline*, 2011. Accessed on August 4, 2013 at http://studentaffairs.com/ejournal/Winter_2001/technophobia.html.

Guthrie, D. MOOCS Are Toast or at Least Should Be. *Forbes*, July 31, 2013. Accessed on August 4, 2013 at http://www.forbes.com/sites/dougguthrie/2013/07/31/moocs-are-toast-or-should-be/.

Hacker, P. Creating Your Web Presence: A Primer for Academics. *Chronicle of Higher Education*, February 14, 2011. Accessed on August 7, 2013 at http://chronicle.com/blogs/profhacker/creating-your-web-presence-a-primer-for-academics/30458.

Havighurst, R. J. *Human Development and Education*. New York: Longmans, Green, 1952.

Higher Education Research Institute. *CIRP Freshmen Survey*. Los Angeles: Author. 2013. Accessed on July 11, 2013 at http://www.heri.ucla.edu/cirpoverview.php.

Hiltzik, M. The Perils of Online College Learning. *Los Angeles Times*, July 26, 2013. Accessed on July 26, 2013 at http://www.latimes.com/business/la-fi-hiltzik-20130728,0,2408536.column.

Hooks, B. *Teaching to Transgress: Education as the Practice of Freedom*. New York: Routledge, 1994.

Huber, M. T., and Hutchings, P. *The Advancement of Learning: Building the Teaching Commons*. A Carnegie Foundation Report on the Scholarship of Teaching and Learning in Higher Education. San Francisco: Jossey-Bass, 2005.

Inside Higher Ed. *Student Affairs and Technology Blog*. 2013. Accessed on August 8, 2013 at http://www.insidehighered.com/blogs/student-affairs-and-technology.

Jacoby, B. (Ed.). *Service Learning in Higher Education: Concepts and Practices*. San Francisco: Jossey-Bass, 1996.

Kang, K. *Branding Pays: The Five-Step System to Reinvent Your Personal Brand*. Palo Alto, CA: BrandingPays Media, 2013.

Keeling, R. (Ed.) *Learning Reconsidered: A Campus-Wide Focus on the Student Experience*. Washington, D.C.: National Association of Student Personnel Administrators and American College Personnel Association, 2004.

Kegan, R. *In Over Our Heads: The Mental Demands of Modern Life*. Cambridge, MA: Harvard University Press, 1994.

Kell, P., and Vogl, G. Transnational Education: The Politics of Mobility, Migration and the Well-Being of International Students. *International Journal of Asia Pacific Studies* 4(1), pp. 21–31, 2008.

Kitchener, K. S. Ethical Principles and Ethical Decisions in Student Affairs. In H. Canon, and R. Brown (Eds.), *Applied Ethics in Student Services.* New Directions for Student Services, #30. San Francisco: Jossey-Bass, 1985.

Knock, G. Development of Student Services in Higher Education. In M. J. Barr, and L. A. Keating (Eds.), *Developing Effective Student Services Programs.* San Francisco: Jossey-Bass, 1985.

Koch, V. A. *An Exploration of Current Practices in Curricular Design of Resident Assistant Training Programs.* Chicago: Loyola University of Chicago, 2012.

Kohlberg, L. *The Development of Modes of Moral Thinking and Choice in the Years Ten to Sixteen.* Chicago: University of Chicago, 1958.

Kohlberg, L. Stages of Moral Development as a Basis for Moral Education. In C. Beck, B. S. Crittendon, and E. V. Sullivan (Eds.), *Moral Education: Interdisciplinary Approaches.* Toronto: University of Toronto Press, 1971.

Kolowich, S. A University's Offer of Credit for a MOOC Gets No Takers. *Chronicle of Higher Education,* July 8, 2013a. Accessed on July 8, 2013 at http://chronicle.com/article/A-Universitys-Offer-of-Credit/140131/.

Kolowich, S. The MOOC "Revolution" May Not Be as Disruptive as Some Had Imagined. *Chronicle of Higher Education,* August 8, 2013b. Accessed on August 8, 2013 at http://chronicle.com/article/MOOCs-May-Not-Be-So-Disruptive/140965/?cid=at andutm_source=at andutm_medium=en.

Kotter, J. P. *Leading Change.* Boston: Harvard Business School Press, 1996.

Kotter, J. P. *A Sense of Urgency.* Boston: Harvard Business School Press, 2008.

Kotter, J. P., and Cohen, D. S. *The Heart of Change: Real-Life Stories of How People Change Their Organizations.* Boston: Harvard Business School Press, 2002.

Kouzes, J. M., and Posner, B. Z. *Credibility: How Leaders Gain and Lose It, and Why People Demand It.* San Francisco: Jossey-Bass, 2011.

Kouzes, J. M., and Posner, B. Z. *The Leadership Challenge: How to Make Extraordinary Things Happen in Organizations* (4th ed.). San Francisco: Jossey-Bass, 2012.

Kruger, K. (Ed.). *Technology in Student Affairs: Supporting Student Learning and Services.* New Directions for Student Services, #112. San Francisco: Jossey-Bass, 2005.

Kruger, K. Technology: Innovations and Implications. In G. S. McClellan, and J. Stringer (Eds.), *The Handbook of Student Affairs Administration* (3rd ed.). San Francisco: Jossey-Bass, 2009.

Kuh, G. D. Guiding Principles for Creating Seamless Learning Environments for Undergraduates. *Journal of College Student Development,* 37(2), 1996.

Kuh, G. D. Organizational Theory. In S. R. Komives, and D. B. Woodard (Eds.), *Services: A Handbook for the Profession* (4th ed.). San Francisco: Jossey-Bass, 2003.

Kuh, G. D., Kinzie, J., Schuh, J. H., and Whitt, E. J. Fostering Student Success in Hard Times. *Change, 43*(4), 2011. Accessed at http://www.changemag.org/Archives/Back%20Issues/2011/July-August%202011/fostering-student-full.html on March 24, 2014.

Larsen, J., and Pasquini, L. *Emerging Technology for Emerging Leaders: Online Tools for Professional Development.* Presented March 2011 at the American College Personnel Association's annual conference in Baltimore, MD. Accessed on August 7, 2013 at http://www.slideshare.net/LauraPasquini/acpa11-learning-network-competencies-for-student-affairs-professionals-resources.

Laster, J. 2 Scholars Examine Cyberbullying Among College Students. *Chronicle of Higher Education,* June 6, 2010. Access on August 4, 2013 at http://chronicle.com/article/2-Scholars-Examine/65766/.

Leduc, B. F. *The Social Media Case Study: Associating with Associations?* Posted August 7, 2011. Accessed on August, 6, 2013 at http://brianfleduc.com/2011/08/07/associating-with-associations/.

Levine, A., and Dean, D. *Generation on a Tightrope: A Portrait of Today's College Students.* San Francisco: Jossey-Bass, 2012.

Linkedin.com. *Building Your Professional Brand.* 2013. Accessed on August 7, 2013 at http://university.linkedin.com/node/43.

Logan, T. J., Gross, L., Junco, R., and Oliver, S. Here, There, and Everywhere. *ACUHO-I Talking Stick 28*(5), 2011. Accessed on August 3, 2013 at http://www.nxtbook.com/nxtbooks/acuho/talkingstick_20110506/#/36.

Love, P. G. Informal Theory: The Ignored Link in Theory-to-Practice. *Journal of College Student Development, 53*(2), 2012.

Love, P. G., and Estanek, S. M. *Rethinking Student Affairs Practice.* San Francisco: Jossey-Bass, 2004.

MacKinnon, F. J. D., Broido, E. M., and Wilson, M. E. Issues in Student Affairs. In F. J. D. MacKinnon (Ed.), *Rentz's Student Affairs Practice in Higher Education* (3rd ed.). Springfield, IL: Charles C. Thomas, 2004.

Madrid, A. Missing People and Others: Joining Together to Expand the Circle. *Change, 2*(3), pp. 54–59, 1988.

Magolda, P. M., and Gross, K. E. *It's All About Jesus! Faith as an Oppositional Subculture.* Sterling, VA: Stylus. 2009.

Martínez Alemán, A. M., and Renn, K. A. *Women in Higher Education: An Encyclopedia.* Santa Barbara, CA: ABC-CLIO, 2002.

Martínez Alemán, A. M., and Wartman, K. L. *Online Social Networking on Campus: Understanding What Matters in Student Culture*. New York: Routledge, 2009.

Martínez Alemán, A. M., and Wartman, K. L. Student Technology Use and Student Affairs Practice. In J. Schuh, S. R. Jones, and S. R. Harper (Eds.), *Student Services: A Handbook for the Profession* (5th ed.). San Francisco: Jossey-Bass, 2011.

Mathews, L. K. *The Dean of Women*. Boston: Houghton Mifflin, 1915.

McClellan, G. S., and Larimore, J. The Changing Student Population. In G. S. McClellan, and J. Stringer (Eds.), *The Handbook of Student Affairs Administration* (3rd ed.). San Francisco: Jossey Bass, 2009.

McClellan, G. S., and Stringer, J. Epilogue: Continuing the Conversation. In G. S. McClellan, and J. Stringer (Eds.), *The Handbook of Student Affairs Administration* (3rd ed.). San Francisco: Jossey Bass, 2009.

McKaig, R. Keynote Address. NASPA Region IV-East Conference, 2009.

Monat, W. R. Role of Student Services: A President's Perspective. In M. J. Barr, and L. A. Keating (Eds.), *Developing Effective Student Services Programs*. San Francisco: Jossey-Bass, 1985.

Moneta, L. Technology and Student Affairs: Redux. In K. Kruger (Ed.), *Technology in Student Affairs: Supporting Student Learning and Services*. New Directions for Student Services, # 112. San Francisco: Jossey-Bass, 2005.

Moore, E. L. (Ed.). *Student Affairs Staff as Teachers*. New Directions for Student Services, #117, 2007. San Francisco: Jossey-Bass.

Moore, E. L., and Marsh, R. S. College Teaching for Student Affairs Professionals. In E. L. Moore (Ed.), *Student Affairs Staff as Teachers*. New Directions for Student Services, #117, 2007. San Francisco: Jossey-Bass.

National Association of Student Personnel Administrators. *Points of View*. Author, 1989.

National Association of Student Personnel Administrators. *Standards for Professional Practice*. Washington, D.C.: Author, 1990.

National Association of Student Personnel Administrators. *The Student Personnel Point of View: Reflections on 75 Years*. (videotape). Washington, D.C.: Author, 2012.

National Association of Student Personnel Administrators. *NASPA Technology Knowledge Community*. 2013. Accessed on August 6, 2013 at http://www.naspa.org/kc/tech/default.cfm.

National Center for Education Statistics. Fast Facts. Washington, D.C.: Author, 2010. Accessed on September 2, 2013 at http://nces.ed.gov/fastfacts/display.asp?id=98.

O'Neill, T. *All Politics Is Local and Other Rules of the Game*. Avon, MA: Adams Media Corporation, 1995.

O'Toole, J. *Leading Change: Overcoming the Ideology of Comfort and the Tyranny Of Custom*. San Francisco: Jossey-Bass, 1995.

Oblinger, D. G., and Oblinger, J. Is It Age or IT: Toward Understanding the Net Generation. In D. G. Oblinger, and J. Oblinger (Eds.), *Educating the Net Generation*. Washington, D.C.: EDUCAUSE, 2005.

Olsen, E. Every Post Is a "Selfie." *Higher Ed Live*. Posted April 30, 2013. Accessed August 7, 2013 at http://higheredlive.com/every-post-is-a-selfie-the-desire-for-social-approval/.

Palmer, G. H. *The Life of Alice Freeman Palmer*. Boston: Houghton Mifflin Co., 1908.

Pappano, L. The Year of the MOOC. *The New York Times*, November 4, 2012.

Patton, L. D., and Harper, S. R. Using Reflection to Reframe Theory-to-Practice in Student Affairs. In G. S. McClellan, and J. Stringer (Eds.), *The Handbook for Student Affairs Administration* (3rd ed.). San Francisco: Jossey-Bass, 2009.

Petry, N. M., and Weinstock, J. Internet Gambling Is Common in College Students and Associated with Poor Mental Health. *American Journal on Addictions*, 16(5), pp. 325–330, 2007.

Quast, L. *Build a Personal Brand, Not Just a Career*. Forbes. 2012. Accessed on August 7, 2013 at http://www.forbes.com/sites/lisaquast/2012/11/19/build-a-personal-brand-not-just-a-career/.

Reason, R. D., and Kimball, E. W. A New Theory-to-Practice Model for Student Affairs: Integrating Scholarship, Context, and Reflection. *Journal of Student Affairs Research and Practice*, 49(4), 359–376, 2012.

Renn, K. Identity Centers: An Idea Whose Time Has Come And Gone? In P. M. Magolda, and M. B. Baxter Magolda, *Contested Issues in Student Affairs: Diverse Perspectives and Respectful Dialogue*. Sterling. VA: Stylus, 2011.

Rhatigan, J. The History and Philosophy of Student Affairs. In M. Barr, and M. Deshler (Eds.), *The Handbook of Student Affairs Administration* (2nd ed.). San Francisco: Jossey-Bass, 2000.

Ribera, T., Fernandez, S., and Gray, M. Considering the Scholarship of Teaching and Learning in Student Affairs. *About Campus*, January/February, 2012.

Rutkosky, P. J. A Multiperspective Analysis on Developing and Maintaining Trust in Senior Student Affairs Leadership. *Journal of Student Affairs Research and Practice*, 50(2) (2013): 171–188.

Sandeen, A. *Making a Difference: Profiles of Successful Student Affairs Leaders*. Washington, D.C.: National Association of Student Personnel Administrators, 2001.

Sandeen, A. Educating the Whole Student: The Growing Academic Importance of Student Affairs. *Change*, 36(3), 2004.

Sandeen, A., and Barr, M. J. *Critical Issues for Student Affairs.* San Francisco: Jossey-Bass, 2006.

Sanford, N. *The American College.* New York: Wiley, 1962.

Sanford, N. *Self and Society: Social Change and Individual Development.* New York: Atherton, 1966.

Schein, E. H. *Organizational Culture and Leadership.* San Francisco: Jossey-Bass. 1985.

Schein, E. H. *Organizational Culture and Leadership* (4th ed.). San Francisco: Jossey-Bass, 2010.

Schuh, J. H., Jones, S. R., and Harper, S. R. *Student Services: A Handbook for the Profession* (5th ed.). San Francisco: Jossey-Bass, 2011.

Scott, W. D. Board of Personnel Administration at Northwestern University. *School and Society*, 44(4), 1936.

Secretarial Notes on Eleventh Annual Conference of Deans and Advisers of Men. Washington, D.C. April 11–13, 1929.

Senge, P. *The Fifth Discipline: The Art and Practice of the Learning Organization.* San Francisco: Jossey-Bass, 2006.

Shotton, H. J., Lowe, S. C., and Waterman, S. J. (Eds.). *Beyond the Asterisk: Understanding Native Students in Higher Education.* Sterling, VA: Stylus, 2013.

Skipper, T. L. *Student Development in the First College Year.* Columbia, SC: University of South Carolina. National Resource Center for the First-Year Experience & Students in Transition, 2005.

Smith, S. D., Salaway, G., and Caruso, J. B. *The ECAR Study of Undergraduate Students and Information Technology*, 2009. Washington, D.C.: EDUCAUSE, 2009. Accessed on August 4, 2013 at http://www.educause.edu/library/resources/ecar-study-undergraduate-students-and-information-technology-2009.

Stoller, E. *Social Media in Student Affairs Professional Development.* Posted September 21, 2008. Accessed on August 6, 2013 at http://ericstoller.com/blog/2008/09/21/student-affairs-technology-to-boldly-go/.

Stoller, E. *Student Affairs Job Search: Personal Branding.* Posted January 5, 2012. Accessed on August 7, 2013 at http://www.insidehighered.com/blogs/student-affairs-job-search-personal-branding.

Stone, B. The Children of Cyberspace: Old Fogies by Their 20s. *New York Times*, January 9, 2010. Accessed on August 7, 2013 at http://www.nytimes.com/2010/01/10/weekinreview/10stone.html?pagewanted=all and_r=0/.

Straumsheim, C. Digital Research, Not Teaching. *Inside Higher Ed*, April 8, 2013. Accessed on August 4, 2013 at http://www.insidehighered.com/news/2013/04/08/study-shows-gap-between-research-use-classroom-adoption-technology.

Student Affairs.com. *The Journal of Technology in Student Affairs*. 2013. Accessed on August 6, 2013 at http://www.studentaffairs.com/ejournal/Summer_2013/.

Student Affairs Women Talk Tech. 2013. Accessed on August 7, 2013 at http://sawomentalktech.com.

Tarantino, K., McDonough, J., and Hua, M. Effects of Student Engagement with Social Media on Student Learning: A Review of Literature. *The Journal of Technology in Student Affairs*. Summer, 2013. Accessed on July 13, 2013 at http://www.studentaffairs.com/ejournal/Summer_2013/EffectsOfStudentEngagementWithSocialMedia.html.

Tierney, W. G. *Building the Responsive Campus: Creating High Performance College and Universities*. Thousand Oaks, CA: Sage Publications, 1999.

United States Department of Education. *History of TRIO Programs*. Washington, D.C.: Author, 2011. Accessed on September 2, 2013 at http://www2.ed.gov/about/offices/list/ope/trio/triohistory.html.

Upcraft, M. L., and Goldsmith, H. Technological Changes in Student Affairs Administration. In M. J. Barr, and M. K. Desler (Eds.), *The Handbook for Student Affairs Administration* (2nd ed.). San Francisco: Jossey-Bass, 2000.

Upcraft, M. L., and Schuh, J. H. *Assessment in Student Affairs: A Guide for Practitioners*. San Francisco: Jossey-Bass, 1996.

Upcraft, M. L., and Terenzini, P. T. Technology. In C. S. Johnson, and H. E. Cheatham (Eds.), *Higher Education Trends in the Next Century: A Research Agenda for Student Success*. Washington, D.C.: American College Personnel Association, pp. 29–34, 1999.

Walsh, J., Frey, G., and Henley, D. Life in the Fast Lane [The Eagles]. *On Hotel California* [record]. West Hollywood, CA: Asylum Records, 1976.

Weber State University. *Student Affairs Technology TechTrivia*. Ogden, UT: Weber State University, 2013. Accessed on August 4, 2013 at http://sat.weber.edu/techtrivia/default.php.

Cases

Brown v. Board Education. 347 U.S. 483, 1954.
Fisher v. University of Texas et. al. 370 U.S., 2013

Statutes

Americans with Disabilities Act of 1990
Civil Rights Act of 1964, Title VI

Education Amendments of 1976
Morrill Act of 1862
Morrill Act of 1890
Omnibus Appropriations Act of 2001
Section 504 of the Rehabilitation Act of 1973

Index